SHANE MARQUIN VAN ROOYEN

The True Patriot Alignment of the Hearts

When True Patriots Align Nations Are Reborn

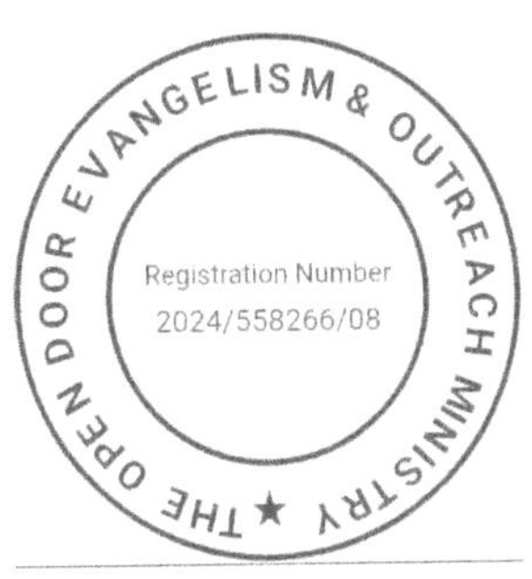

To the South African Nation 🇿🇦

To the land that carries our blood and dreams,
to the soil that has felt both our tears and our triumphs,
to the mountains that have heard our prayers,
and to the oceans that have carried our hope —

This book is for you,
the Nation of South Africa.

To every mother who still believes in her child,
to every father who works through struggle and silence,
to every youth who dares to dream beyond poverty.

Contents

Foreword

To my brothers and sisters in the Patriotic Alliance, serving in green
  to every son and daughter of this land,
  and to every believer in the rebirth of South Africa —
  this book is written from the deepest part of my heart.

A Vision Born from Love

When I first began to write The True Patriot, I did not set out to create a political book.

I set out to write a spiritual journey — one that speaks to the heart of humanity, the heart of South Africa, and the heart of God's purpose for this nation.

For too long, our people — especially the Coloured Nation, the descendants of the Khoisan — have carried pain in silence.

We were made to feel invisible in the very land of our ancestors.

But God has always had His eye on the forgotten, and He never writes anyone out of His story.

Through the rising of the Patriotic Alliance, He began to awaken something ancient and divine —
  the spirit of true patriotism.

This movement, though misunderstood by many, is not just a party.
  It is a calling.

It is the gathering of a people whose hearts burn for truth, justice, and unity — a family of believers who see beyond colour, beyond class, beyond status.

To the Leader — The True Patriot

To President Gayton McKenzie,
    this book honours your journey —
    not as a politician, but as a patriot of the heart.

You have stood where many fell.
    You have spoken when silence was safer.
    You have served when comfort was easier.

Your courage has given hope to millions,
    and your compassion has proven that leadership is not power — it is purpose.
    You have become a living example of what it means to carry the heart of a true patriot.

This book captures the spirit of that journey — the calling to unite, to restore, and to serve all South Africans.
    Through storms and victories, criticism and celebration,
    you have remained steadfast to the mission:
    to see South Africa healed from its deepest wounds.

May history remember you not only as a leader,
    but as a rebuilder of hearts.

To the Members and Supporters

To every member of the Patriotic Alliance, every volunteer, every
believer who wears green with pride —
    you are more than followers of a movement;
    you are keepers of a vision.

This book is your reflection.
    It tells the story of your faith, your fight, your forgiveness.
    It reminds the world that patriotism is not politics — it is personal.
    It begins with love, and it ends with unity.

When you feed a hungry neighbour,
    when you speak peace in a divided place,
    when you stand up for what is right —
    you are the embodiment of this message.

You are the heartbeat of this new South Africa.

To the People of South Africa

This book is not just for one party, one race, or one class.
    It is for every South African —
    for the worker, the mother, the youth, the elder, the dreamer.

Because being a patriot does not belong to any political structure —
    it belongs to the human spirit.
    It belongs to every person who dares to believe that goodness still
lives in this nation.

Let this book remind us that we are not enemies —
    we are family.
    And though our differences may be many,

our destiny is one.

To Humanity

Beyond South Africa, this book speaks to the soul of the world.
    It is a message of alignment —
    a call for nations to return to compassion,
    for leaders to return to service,
    and for hearts to return to God.

If we can learn to see one another through love,
    we will no longer live as strangers,
    but as stewards of a shared destiny.

For the true patriot is not born from politics —
    but from purpose.

From My Heart to Yours

To the readers, the dreamers, the believers,
    I offer this book as a gift of hope.
    It was written in prayer, with faith that one day the world will understand
    that South Africa's story is not one of defeat — it is one of divine rebirth.

May every chapter remind you that your life matters.
    That you were born for this time, for this nation, for this calling.
    And that when your heart aligns with God's heart,
    you too become a true patriot.

Let this be your declaration:

"I will love my people.
  I will serve my land.
  I will align my heart with truth."

And together, we will see the fulfillment of the promise:
  that the land will remember her children,
  and the children will remember their purpose.

With honour, faith, and gratitude,
  ✍ Shane Marquin van Rooyen
  Author of The True Patriot: Alignment of the Hearts
  South Africa 🇿🇦

Preface

Preface

By Shane Marquin van Rooyen

There are moments in life when a nation's destiny calls louder than any voice of fear.

Moments when the heart of a people must awaken — not through politics, but through purpose.

The True Patriot: Alignment of the Hearts was born out of such a moment.

This book is not written from theory or ambition; it is written from **conviction**.

It is the story of faith, identity, and unity — of a people long overlooked, yet never forgotten by God.

It is the echo of the Khoisan heritage, the heartbeat of the coloured nation, and the cry of a generation rising to reclaim their rightful place in history.

In the pages that follow, you will find the story of **true patriotism** — not as the world defines it, but as Heaven reveals it.

You will see how one man's obedience to God's call, **Minister Gayton McKenzie**, became a living symbol of what it means to love one's country with a pure heart.

His leadership, compassion, and courage reflect what happens when a man aligns his heart with the will of God and stands as a light for his people.

This book is a message to **all South Africans**, but especially to the youth — the builders of tomorrow.

It calls you to see beyond division, beyond history, beyond pain — and to look toward alignment, reconciliation, and rebirth.

It invites you to rediscover the power that lies within unity and the beauty that shines through diversity.

We are not writing a story of politics.

We are recording a movement of hearts.

A movement that says, "We are one people under one God, in one land, with one destiny."

The vision of the Patriotic Alliance stands as a reflection of this truth — that South Africa belongs to all who love it, protect it, and serve it with humility.

The True Patriot is the one who stands even when misunderstood, who loves even when rejected, and who continues to serve even when opposed.

To be a True Patriot is to put **God first**, people second, and self last.

It is to see your nation not as a battlefield, but as a garden ready to bloom again.

And it is to understand that this calling is not for a season — it is **for generations**.

So I invite you, reader — open your heart as you open these pages.

Let the Spirit of alignment flow through you.

Let God awaken the patriot within you.

Because when true patriots align, **nations are reborn.**

Salut. 🇿🇦

— *Shane Marquin van Rooyen*

Author of *The True Patriot: Alignment of the Hearts*

Founder — Open Door Evangelism & Outreach Ministry, South Africa

Acknowledgments

With a heart full of gratitude

Every book is a journey, and no journey is ever walked alone.
   This one, especially, was written not only with ink but with the voices,
hearts, and prayers of a nation that still believes in hope.

First, I give all glory to God Almighty,
   the Author of all creation,
   the One who gave me vision, courage, and breath to complete this
work.
   Without His grace, this book — and my life — would have no purpose.

To my family, who stood by me through every late night and long day
—
   thank you for your patience, your faith, and your love that never gave
up on me.
   You are my greatest blessing and my daily reason to keep going.

To the Patriotic Alliance — my brothers and sisters in the movement of
unity —
   thank you for your boldness, your love for South Africa,
   and your commitment to lifting up the forgotten communities of this
land.
   You are the living proof that patriotism is not about division but about

devotion.

To President Gayton McKenzie,
   a man whose courage has inspired millions and whose heart beats for
the people —
   thank you for reminding us that leadership is service, not status.
   Your journey from struggle to service has become a light to many,
   and your example gave birth to this message: the heart of a true patriot
still beats in South Africa.

To every community leader, mother, youth, and elder
   who shared their stories, tears, and dreams with me along the way —
   this book is your testimony too.
   You reminded me that patriotism is found not in speeches but in
everyday acts of love, sacrifice, and faith.

To the readers — every person who opens these pages —
   thank you for believing in South Africa.
   Thank you for believing that unity is still possible,
   that healing can still come,
   and that the heart of this nation can beat again with pride and purpose.

Finally, to my friends and supporters across the country —
   from the townships to the cities,
   from the farms to the classrooms —
   you are the reason this message exists.
   Never stop believing in who we are.
   Never stop praying for our land.
   And never stop walking in the spirit of a True Patriot.

Introduction

Becoming a True Patriot of Heart

"Before a nation can rise, its people must remember how to love."

The world today is restless.

Nations are divided, hearts are cold, and truth seems to fade beneath the noise of politics and pride. Everywhere you look, there is conflict — between people, between classes, between colours, between creeds. Humanity has forgotten the sacred rhythm of unity.

But from the south of Africa, a heartbeat begins to rise again — slow, steady, and sure.

It is the heartbeat of patriotism reborn.

Not the shallow kind that waves flags for fame or fights only for power —

but the true patriotism that flows from a heart aligned with love, justice, and purpose.

This book is a journey into that heartbeat.

It is not only the story of a movement or a man — it is the awakening of a generation.

It is the story of people rediscovering who they are in the eyes of God and in the soil of their birth.

The Call to Humanity

Every person is born with a place of belonging.
But belonging is more than where you live — it's what you live for.
The heart of a true patriot beats for others. It serves without expectation.
It builds bridges where others build walls.
It stands firm in storms, not because of pride, but because of purpose.

To be a true patriot of heart is to say:

"I will not abandon my nation in its weakness.
I will strengthen it with my love."

The world does not need more politicians or preachers — it needs patriots of the heart.
Men and women who see beyond race, religion, and region.
People who fight not for position, but for peace.
Who speak truth even when it is costly,
and who lead not with arrogance, but with alignment.

The Rebirth of a People

This book rises from the soil of South Africa —
a land of colour, conflict, and calling.
It tells the story of the Coloured Nation, descendants of the First People — the Khoisan — whose history was buried beneath centuries of struggle.
A people of many bloodlines, yet one soul.
A people chosen not by chance, but by destiny to become the living bridge between races,

and the foundation of a new South African identity.

Through pain, they learned patience.
Through rejection, they discovered resilience.
And through faith, they found rebirth.

The Example of a True Patriot

Every movement has a messenger.
In the modern story of South Africa, that messenger is Gayton McKenzie —
a man who rose from hardship to leadership, from brokenness to belief.

But this book is not about his fame — it is about his heart.
For in his journey we see what a true patriot really looks like:
one who loves his people more than position,
who stands firm against lies and opposition,
and who believes that the only real victory is when all South Africans win together.

Gayton's story reflects a greater truth — that when a person's heart aligns with God's vision,
he or she becomes unstoppable.
And when a nation's heart aligns with that same truth,
the impossible becomes inevitable.

The Alignment of the Hearts

The phrase "Alignment of the Hearts" is not political — it is prophetic.
It means the coming together of souls who share one divine rhythm:

to serve, to heal, to uplift.

This alignment begins within each of us.
Before a country can change, the citizen must change.
Before a government can be just, the heart must be pure.
Before a flag can stand for unity, the people must first learn to forgive.

When the human heart aligns with heaven, nations heal from the inside out.
And that is the message of this book —
that patriotism is not just about where you live,
but how you love.

A Message to the World

Though this story is born in South Africa, its message belongs to the world.
Every nation has its wounds.
Every people have their divisions.
But within every generation, there rises a remnant —
men and women whose hearts burn for truth and peace.

If you are reading this, perhaps that calling is yours.

You may not hold a title, wear a uniform, or speak from a podium.
But you can still be a true patriot —
in your family, in your school, in your community, in your art, in your prayer.

You can carry the spirit of unity wherever you go.
You can speak hope into the hopeless.

You can choose alignment over anger.
You can love your people even when it is hard to.

The Journey Ahead

The pages that follow will take you on a journey —
from the ancient soil of the Khoisan, through the rebirth of the Coloured nation,
to the rise of modern South Africa under new leadership and divine vision.

You will walk through pain and prophecy, politics and purpose,
until you arrive at the greatest revelation of all:
that the future belongs to those who love their nation enough to serve it with clean hands and a humble heart.

Final Reflection

This book is a mirror.
When you reach the end, you will see yourself reflected —
not as a spectator of history, but as a participant in destiny.

For the true patriot is not found in government buildings or on campaign stages.
The true patriot is the mother who feeds her neighbour's child,
the teacher who believes in the forgotten student,
the artist who sings of peace,
the believer who prays for the land every night.

This is the alignment of the hearts.
This is how nations are reborn.

This is how humanity becomes whole again.

Welcome to the journey.
You are about to discover not just the story of a people —
but the heartbeat of a world ready to heal.

This is The True Patriot.
This is the Alignment of the Hearts.

Chapter 1 — The First People

"Before the names of nations, there was a heartbeat in the dust."

Long before borders, flags, or politics, there was a people who walked the earth with bare feet and clean hearts. They spoke to the wind and the water, and they knew the land not as property, but as mother. These were the Khoisan, the First People — the original custodians of Southern Africa, whose stories were whispered into the stones and the stars.

Their footprints are the oldest in the world, pressed deep into the red sands of the Karoo, the dunes of the Kalahari, and the cliffs of the Cape. Their laughter once echoed through the valleys where today the cities rise. Before time was counted in calendars and empires, the Khoisan already knew the rhythm of the seasons, the secrets of healing herbs, the language of the antelope and the rain.

They did not write history with ink; they carved it into memory.

They sang it through generations, in the clicking beauty of their tongues.

They were the heartbeat of creation's dawn.

The Land and the Covenant

To the Khoisan, the land was sacred — a covenant between the Creator and His children. Each sunrise was a promise, each sunset a prayer. They hunted not for greed but for gratitude. They built communities where no one went hungry, where wisdom was passed through stories told under the firelight.

In their simplicity, they carried something modern civilization often forgets — harmony. They lived by balance, knowing that to wound the land was to wound themselves. This truth, passed through bloodlines, would one day become the seed of a new patriotism: love for the land, and respect for all who live upon it.

The Arrival of Strangers

Then came the ships — sails white against the blue horizon. Strangers stepped onto the sacred shore. They brought strange languages, strange gods, and strange desires. What began as trade turned into takeover; what began as friendship became the theft of land and identity.

The Khoisan fought bravely, but their spears were no match for muskets. Their cattle were taken, their rivers renamed, their language silenced. The first people became the forgotten people. Yet even in their loss, they carried something no conqueror could take — the memory of belonging.

They watched as other nations came — slaves from the East, settlers from Europe, tribes from the north. Bloods mixed, cultures intertwined, and a new people were born from the ashes — the Coloured Nation, descendants of many, but children of one soil.

The People of Many Bloods

From the pain of the past, a miracle emerged.

A people not defined by colour, but by courage.

Not by division, but by divine design.

The Coloured nation became the living bridge of South Africa — carrying African, Asian, and European roots in one heartbeat. In their veins flowed the blood of all races, the song of many languages, and the laughter of survivors.

They were not "in-between." They were the link — proof that God can create unity through diversity. The forgotten people had become the reflection of every South African story, the DNA of the nation itself.

The Hidden Prophecy

Elders spoke of a time when the first people's descendants would rise again — not in rebellion, but in revelation.

They said: "The land will remember its children. And when they stand again, the heart of Africa will beat anew."

That prophecy lingered in the air for centuries, waiting for its appointed time.

For generations, the Coloured nation carried that promise quietly — through struggle, through laughter, through prayer. And in the fullness of time, a new voice would rise — a man who carried that ancient fire, whose heart beat in rhythm with the ancestors and aligned with God's vision for a reborn South Africa.

That man would be called a True Patriot.

Closing Reflection

The story of a patriot begins not with politics, but with roots — with knowing who you are and whose land you stand upon. To love your nation, you must first love its story, even the painful chapters.

For in the dust of the first people lies the key to South Africa's healing:
A nation cannot rise until it honours its origins.
And those origins begin here — with the Khoisan, the first dreamers of Africa.

Chapter 2 — The Blood of Many Colours

"We are the children of the soil — shaped by every sun that ever rose over Africa."

When the first people were scattered by conquest and colonization, something unexpected began to form — a new kind of nation, woven from the threads of many origins.

It was not born from one tribe or tongue, but from a meeting of histories, a divine blending that the world struggled to define but Heaven understood.

This was the Coloured Nation — the children of many bloods — and their story is the story of South Africa itself.

The Meeting of Bloodlines

In the Cape of Good Hope, worlds collided.

Europe met Africa.

The East met the West.

Slaves, settlers, and sons of the soil shared the same horizon, the same air, and eventually — the same blood.

Portuguese explorers brought Malays and Indians from the East. Dutch settlers came with ambition and power. African tribes migrated from the north. And in the midst of this mixture stood the Khoisan — the first witnesses of it all.

Over generations, these bloodlines intertwined — not always in peace, but in fate. From pain and survival, a new people emerged. They were called many things — "Bastaards," "Brown," "Half-castes." But they carried a beauty far beyond the names given to them.

They were the reflection of all humanity's colours in one face.

The Birth of a Bridge Nation

The Coloured people became the bridge between worlds that often refused to meet.
    They spoke multiple languages — Afrikaans, English, Xhosa, Tswana, Nama — and walked easily between communities.
    They were born of diversity, yet taught to choose sides in a divided land.

But the truth is: they were never meant to choose.
    They were meant to connect.
    To stand as living proof that unity is not an idea — it is blood-deep.

This nation of bridges carried in its DNA every race that ever set foot on South African soil. Within them, the African drum, the European violin, and the Eastern gong all played in one symphony.

Forgotten but Faithful

History tried to erase them.

Governments categorized them.
The world misunderstood them.

And yet, through all of this, they remained faithful.
Faithful to God.
Faithful to family.
Faithful to the idea that tomorrow could be better.

In the Cape flats, in the Karoo dust, in the townships of Gqeberha and Kimberly, this nation kept its humour alive. They turned pain into poetry, struggle into song, and survival into art. They made something beautiful out of brokenness.

They worked in the kitchens, built the railways, played on dusty soccer fields, and sang gospel in the streets. They raised their children to believe in something greater — "Work hard, stay humble, trust God."

They had little, but gave much.
They were counted out, but never gave up.

The Blood That Remembers

Every generation carries a spiritual memory.
For the Coloured people, that memory is sacred: a connection to the First People, a sense that the soil itself recognizes them.

They may have been labeled and misplaced by governments, but the land never forgot them. When they walk barefoot across the veld, the earth knows its children. The wind knows their songs.

The Blood of Many Colours is not a mark of confusion — it is a mark of calling.

A calling to unity.

A calling to healing.

A calling to patriotism that sees every race as family.

The Spiritual Meaning of Colour

In God's creation, colour was never meant to divide.

Each shade of skin is a reflection of His artistry. The rainbow was His signature — a covenant of promise. And so it is with the Coloured nation: the living rainbow of South Africa.

When a nation learns to honour its colours, it honours its Creator.

When it rejects those colours, it rejects a part of itself.

The Coloured people carry within them the code for reconciliation — not just social or political reconciliation, but spiritual rebirth. They are the reminder that no one is "half." We are all whole, because we were made in God's image.

From Forgotten to Found

It would take generations — centuries even — for the world to understand what the Coloured nation truly represents. But every era produces a voice that awakens the sleeping truth.

In time, one such voice would rise — bold, unafraid, and rooted in both pain and promise. He would remind South Africans that being Coloured was not a curse, but a calling. He would carry the courage of the Khoisan, the compassion of a servant, and the conviction of a leader chosen for his time.

His name would echo across communities and continents — Gayton McKenzie — a man whose story would prove that the Blood of Many Colours still beats strong, still dreams, still believes.

Closing Reflection

South Africa's heart is not divided — it is layered.
    Each layer tells a story, and every story matters.

To understand patriotism, one must first understand identity.
    And to understand identity, one must embrace every colour within it.

The Blood of Many Colours is not the story of a people lost — it is the story of a nation waiting to find itself again.

Chapter 3 — The Broken Voice

"They took our land, but not our song."

The heart of a people can survive almost anything — hunger, exile, even war.

But the deepest wound of all is to be unheard.

For centuries, the descendants of the First People — the Coloured Nation — carried that wound: a broken voice in the land that birthed them.

Silenced by Systems

When the colonizers came, they didn't only claim the land — they claimed the right to tell its story.

The Khoisan were written out of the record, renamed, and reclassified.

The mixed descendants who came after were placed in a box — "Coloured" — a term meant to categorize, not to celebrate.

They were told:

"You are not black enough. You are not white enough. You belong nowhere."

That was the cruel lie of the system — to make a people question their belonging in their own homeland.

And yet, beneath the silence, something sacred remained: the heart-beat of memory.

A People Between Worlds

Generation after generation, the Coloured people lived between worlds.

They spoke the language of the powerful but lived with the poor.

They worked in the fields, in the kitchens, and in the mines — invisible architects of a nation that never acknowledged them.

In schools, their history was erased.

In politics, their voices were sidelined.

Even in freedom struggles, they were often forgotten.

They were present everywhere, yet mentioned nowhere.

Still, they loved their country.

Still, they prayed for rain when drought came.

Still, they raised their children to dream higher than their circum-stances.

Songs in the Silence

When you take away a people's right to speak, they learn to sing.

In the Coloured communities of the Cape and beyond, songs became the language of survival.

The hymns sung in church halls, the jazz that rose from District Six, the ghoema rhythms that made the streets dance — these were not entertainment; they were endurance.

Every melody was a memory.
  Every drumbeat said, "We are still here."

Through music, they remembered what history tried to bury.
  Through storytelling, they kept their roots alive.
  Through laughter, they refused to die in despair.

They turned brokenness into brilliance.
  Pain became poetry. Silence became strength.

The Long Shadow of Apartheid

Then came the long night — Apartheid.
  A system designed to divide, to rank human worth by colour, to strip away dignity.
  For the Coloured Nation, it was a time of confusion and contradiction.

They were given crumbs of privilege compared to others, but still denied humanity.
  They could not vote. They could not live freely. They could not dream openly.
  The system wanted obedience, not identity.

Families were uprooted.
  Communities like District Six were bulldozed to the ground.
  Churches, schools, and memories vanished in the dust.

But you cannot bulldoze a spirit.
  You cannot exile a people from their purpose.
  The harder the oppression, the louder the silent prayer:
  "One day, our story will be told again."

Faith in the Fire

Every grandmother who whispered scripture over her children kept the nation's soul alive.

Every father who went to work at dawn with calloused hands and tired eyes built hope into the soil.

Every child who grew up on faith alone became a seed for the next generation.

The Coloured people's greatest weapon was never violence — it was faith.

Faith that God saw what history ignored.

Faith that the heart of the nation would one day be healed.

It was that faith that carried them through.

It was that faith that kept the bloodlines pure in purpose, even when names and languages faded.

The Awakening Beneath the Ashes

But even while they were silenced, history was shifting.

The blood of many colours could not be denied forever.

From the ashes of dispossession rose a quiet pride, a realization that being "in between" was not a curse — it was a calling.

The Coloured nation began to rediscover its roots.

They found traces of the Khoisan in their DNA, in their mannerisms, in their music, in their faith.

They began to see that they were not forgotten — they were hidden for a season.

And when that season ended, a new voice would rise — a voice that would not whisper anymore, but declare:

"This is our land too. This is our story too. We are part of the heart of South Africa."

The Voice Returns

That voice would not come from politics first, but from patriotism — from a love for the people, for the nation, for God's vision of unity.

And when it did rise, it would carry generations of silence inside it — a thunder built from centuries of whispers.

In time, that voice would be embodied by a man who refused to be silent, who stood up for his people, not through anger, but through purpose.

His name would echo through the broken valleys and forgotten towns, saying:

"You are not invisible.
You are the foundation of this land.
You are the true patriots."

That man was Gayton McKenzie — the return of the voice that history tried to bury.

Closing Reflection

Silence may last for a season, but truth lasts forever.
A people's story can be delayed, but never destroyed.

The broken voice of the Coloured Nation is rising again — stronger, prouder, and aligned with divine purpose.

For every time they were silenced, God was only tuning their song. And now, the world is beginning to listen.

Chapter 4 — The Heart That Never Forgot

Chapter 4 — The Heart That Never Forgot

"You can strip a people of everything, except the memory of who they are."

There are nations that rise through power, and others that rise through pain.

The Coloured Nation of South Africa rose through heart.

Though they were pushed aside, renamed, and written out of their own story, they carried within them something that no system could erase — memory.

It lived in their music, in their faith, in their laughter, and in the quiet strength of their homes.

It was the pulse of a people who refused to forget where they came from.

A Flame in the Darkness

Long after the colonizers left and the headlines changed, the ordinary Coloured man and woman kept a flame burning — small but steady.

In humble kitchens filled with the smell of fried fish and koesisters, they prayed for their children.

In cramped backyards, they raised their families with dignity.

In laughter that echoed down the lanes of Hanover Park, Mitchells Plain, or the dusty towns of Upington and Beaufort West, they found ways to make life beautiful, even when it was hard.

They did not wait for government or miracles.

They became their own miracle — resourceful, determined, and alive with faith.

When the world forgot them, they remembered themselves.

That is the strength of a people who carry memory in their blood.

Faith Was Their Fortress

When you walked into a Coloured home, you often found a worn Bible sitting on the table, its pages filled with notes, tears, and hope.

Faith was not a Sunday costume — it was a daily meal.

When rent was due, they prayed.

When sickness came, they prayed.

When the world seemed to turn against them, they still prayed — and then they sang.

Churches became more than places of worship. They became schools of survival, sanctuaries of song, and spaces of healing.

The voices that rose from those pews were more powerful than any protest — because they sang from faith, not fury.

They believed that if they stayed true, God would one day lift them up again.

Their faith became their fortress, and through it, their identity remained untouched.

Laughter as Resistance

Where others would have grown bitter, the Coloured Nation grew funny.
   Humour was their rebellion.
   They could turn pain into a punchline, and hardship into a story that made the whole street laugh.

That laughter was not denial — it was defiance with dignity.
   It was a way of saying:

"You can take everything, but you won't take our joy."

This joy became their greatest inheritance.
   Even in times of scarcity, they made something from nothing — a feast out of scraps, a celebration out of survival.
   Where there was despair, they made music.
   Where there was sorrow, they made dance.
   They transformed endurance into art.

Ubuntu in Action

In a world divided by colour and class, Coloured communities lived Ubuntu without ever naming it.
   If one neighbour cooked, the smell travelled through the entire street — because everyone would taste.
   If one family suffered, another stepped in.
   When funerals came, the entire block gathered to comfort and cook.
   When weddings came, everyone danced.

They lived by an unspoken law: no one is left behind.

Ubuntu — "I am because we are" — was not philosophy for them; it was survival.

This is what kept the community alive when resources were few and recognition was none.

It was not the government that sustained them.

It was compassion, the purest form of patriotism.

The Songs That Remembered

Every generation carried its own sound.

The ghoema drum of Cape Town.

The harmonies of the church choirs.

The jazz that drifted through District Six before it was torn down.

Through melody, memory lived on.

Every song told a story of identity, of belonging, of being more than a label.

Even when their voices were excluded from national anthems, their music filled the streets — proclaiming, "We are still here."

Those songs became prophecies in rhythm, preparing a nation for a rebirth still to come.

The Unbroken Line

The heart of the Coloured Nation never forgot because it was never truly separated from its origins.

The blood of the Khoisan still ran through their veins, carrying ancient wisdom and connection to the land.

The spirit of the first people lived on in their resilience, in their humour, in their faith.

And that same spirit began to stir again — quietly, powerfully — as if the land itself was remembering.

For every time the Coloured Nation laughed, loved, or prayed, the soil whispered back:

"My children are waking up."

A people that remember who they are cannot remain silent forever.

The heart that never forgot was being prepared — for alignment, for purpose, for leadership.

The Rise of a True Patriot

Then came a man whose life embodied that same memory — a man of faith, courage, and conviction.

He rose not from the comfortable halls of privilege, but from the streets where that laughter, pain, and faith were born.

His journey echoed the story of his people: rejected, refined, and reborn.

That man was Gayton McKenzie.

He carried in his voice the same rhythm as the ancestors, the same humour as the people, and the same heart that never forgot.

He did not rise to divide, but to remind.

He stood not as a politician, but as a patriot — one whose heart beats in alignment with the land and the will of God.

In him, the forgotten found a voice again.

In him, the laughter and the prayers of generations found a purpose.

Closing Reflection

The heart that never forgot has now begun to lead.

It beats inside every South African who still believes in hope.

It is the proof that love outlasts injustice, that faith outlives systems, and that memory outshines lies.

To be a true patriot is to carry that same heart — the heart that remembers where it came from, and believes in what can still be.

For as long as that heart beats, South Africa still has a chance to rise again.

Chapter 5 — The Spirit of Ubuntu

"**A** true patriot does not rise above his people; he rises among them."

The Invisible Thread

Ubuntu is more than a word — it is the heartbeat of South Africa.

It is the invisible thread that binds people together through compassion, respect, and shared humanity.

For generations, even before the term was known, the Coloured Nation and the broader South African family lived it naturally.

When the world looked away, they turned to one another.

When resources ran out, they shared what little they had.

Ubuntu was not something they spoke — it was something they became.

A pot of food never fed one household; it fed the whole street.

A celebration was never private; it was community.

Sorrow was never faced alone; it was carried together.

This was the silent code of survival and love that shaped the moral backbone of a forgotten nation.

A Heritage of Humanity

In every township, in every rural settlement, there are stories that prove Ubuntu lives.

A neighbour sharing paraffin when the lights go out.

An auntie feeding children that aren't her own.

A stranger stopping to pray for someone in distress.

This is the South Africa that does not make the news — the one built from kindness, from shared pain, from hope.

Ubuntu was born in huts and homes long before it became a slogan.

It was taught through actions, not speeches.

And through it, God revealed something powerful — that love is the greatest weapon against oppression.

The Forgotten Carriers

Many do not realise that the Coloured Nation were among the strongest carriers of Ubuntu in daily life.

They carried multiple cultures in their veins — Khoisan, African, European, Asian — and instead of division, they embodied connection.

They were bridges where others built walls.

They knew the struggle of every side, and yet they held no hatred.

That is the essence of Ubuntu: to love even when you have been denied love.

To forgive even when you have been forgotten.

To build even when your own foundation was broken.

The Coloured people lived that truth daily — a living lesson for a nation in need of unity.

Ubuntu and Patriotism

Ubuntu and patriotism are twins of the same heart.
    Ubuntu says, "I am because we are."
    Patriotism says, "I live to see my nation thrive."
    One cannot exist without the other.

A true patriot is not one who only waves a flag or sings an anthem.
    A true patriot is one who lives for others — who works to heal, uplift, and unite.
    Ubuntu turns patriotism from pride into purpose.

This is what Gayton McKenzie understood when he began speaking to the people — not as a politician, but as a brother, a son, a servant of his nation.
    He saw Ubuntu not as a memory of the past but as the blueprint for South Africa's rebirth.

The Reawakening

As Gayton travelled across towns and provinces, he didn't speak the language of division; he spoke the language of family.
    He said, "We are one people. We are all South Africans. Let us build together."

And people listened — not because of his power, but because of his heart.
    In him, they saw a man who had lived the struggle, who had walked the streets they walked, who had felt the hunger they felt.

He didn't come to rule them; he came to remind them — that greatness lives inside their unity.

His leadership reminded people that Ubuntu is the foundation of true patriotism.
When one rises, all must rise.
When one suffers, all must care.
When one succeeds, all must celebrate.

This is the dream that built the Patriotic Alliance — a movement not of politics, but of people.
A colourful alliance, made of every race, every tongue, every heart that still believes in South Africa's potential.

Ubuntu in Action

When Gayton became the Minister of Sport, Arts, and Culture, he didn't come with empty promises — he came with a mission:
to give every South African a chance to shine.

He poured resources into the forgotten corners — rural schools, community teams, small-town artists.
He revived sports fields and restored cultural programs.
He opened doors for those long shut out of opportunity.

Under his leadership, Ubuntu became visible.
It wasn't just words anymore — it was action.
Athletes from poor communities got funding.
Artists who had been silenced were given platforms.
Cultural festivals that once died out began to breathe again.

For the first time in many years, South Africans saw miracles — not supernatural ones, but national ones.

Miracles of unity.

Miracles of fairness.

Miracles of a government that remembered the people.

The True Spirit of Ubuntu

Ubuntu teaches us that humanity cannot be divided by race or status.

We are one creation, designed by one Creator, called to love one another.

That truth lives in the vision of a true patriot — a person who looks beyond the boundaries of skin and language and sees the shared heartbeat of a nation.

Gayton often said, "Let us build a South Africa where no child goes hungry, where no artist is forgotten, where no sport field is empty."

That dream is Ubuntu in motion.

That dream is patriotism in its purest form.

From Streets to Nation

In every street, from Eldorado Park to Bishop Lavis, from Gqeberha to Kimberley, a new sound is rising — the sound of alignment.

People are beginning to realise that the future will not be built by government alone, but by us — ordinary citizens who live Ubuntu daily.

When communities stand together, they become unbreakable.

When they work together, they become unstoppable.

And when they believe together, they become a nation reborn.

Closing Reflection

The Spirit of Ubuntu is the Spirit of God — love made visible through people.
It teaches us that no patriot can stand alone.
To love one's country is to love its people — all of them.

Ubuntu is the secret ingredient in the heart of a true patriot.
It is what turns leadership into service, and service into legacy.
It is what keeps the flame of hope alive, even in dark times.

When Ubuntu and Patriotism meet, alignment happens.
And when alignment happens, a nation is reborn.

Chapter 6 — The Rebirth of the People

"A nation is not reborn through power, but through purpose."

The Awakening

Every generation has a moment when something inside them shifts — a spiritual awakening that cannot be explained by politics or policy.

It's not just change; it's rebirth.

Across South Africa, in dusty towns and crowded cities, that awakening began quietly.

People started to speak differently — not as victims, but as victors.

They started to see themselves not as outcasts, but as carriers of legacy.

It was as if the soul of the nation had heard a call — and was finally answering.

That call was the voice of true patriotism — a voice that said:

"You are more than what you've been told.

You are the children of this soil.

You are the heartbeat of this land."

And slowly, the people began to rise.

The Forgotten Remembered

For too long, the Coloured Nation — the descendants of the Khoisan, the first people of this land — had been left out of the national story.
They had shed blood for a land that did not honour their name.
They had laboured for freedom that often overlooked their contribution.
Yet, through it all, they held on to something sacred — memory and faith.

Now, as the spirit of patriotism moved across the land, that memory began to breathe again.
The people started remembering who they were.
They began to reclaim their pride — not arrogance, but ancestral dignity.
They began to stand taller, speak louder, and dream bigger.

Because when a people remember who they are, their destiny can no longer be denied.

The Role of Prophecy

Every true movement carries the whisper of divine prophecy.
South Africa's rebirth was never meant to come from division, but from alignment — a spiritual realignment of heart and purpose.

Prophets long ago spoke of a day when the first people would rise again, not to rule, but to restore balance — to remind the nation of its soul.
They would rise not with weapons, but with wisdom.

Not through rebellion, but through reconciliation.

And in the unfolding of history, a leader emerged whose heart matched the prophecy — Gayton McKenzie.
He didn't come wearing a crown; he came carrying a calling.
He became a vessel through which God began to realign the hearts of a broken nation.

The Leader of Rebirth

When Gayton spoke, people listened — not because he demanded authority, but because he carried authenticity.
He spoke like someone who knew both pain and promise.
He didn't promise paradise; he promised participation.
He reminded people that rebirth is not given — it is chosen.

He said:

"We cannot wait for others to fix what we were born to restore.
We must build our own table, raise our own children, and write our own history."

And those words ignited something powerful.
Communities began to organize themselves again.
Young people began to dream again.
The Coloured Nation — long ignored — began to believe again.

This was the rebirth of the people.
Not a revolution of anger, but a revolution of identity.

The Power of Unity

The Patriotic Alliance was never meant to be a party of exclusion — it was a movement of inclusion.

Its base was the Coloured Nation, yes, but its vision was for all South Africans.

Black, White, Indian, Coloured — all are part of one story, one land, one destiny.

It stood as proof that unity is not found in sameness, but in alignment of purpose.

When hearts align, colour fades.

When hearts align, healing begins.

When hearts align, the impossible becomes possible.

That is the miracle of rebirth — when people who once stood apart begin to stand together.

The Return to the Land

Part of rebirth is returning to the soil that gave you life.

The Khoisan understood this truth long before borders and politics.

They believed the land was sacred — a living inheritance from God.

Now, that same belief began to stir again.

Communities started cultivating land, reviving traditional farming, reconnecting youth with their heritage.

They understood that owning the land meant more than title deeds — it meant knowing who you are and where you come from.

Rebirth meant not just owning South Africa's land, but healing it — restoring respect for creation and responsibility for one another.

The Spirit of the Young

Every rebirth needs the energy of youth.
And in this movement, young people began to find their voice again.
No longer content to just watch, they began to work, create, serve, and speak.

From arts and sports to business and innovation, they became the new heartbeat of the Patriotic spirit.
They didn't wait for permission — they acted on purpose.
They saw Gayton not as a distant figure, but as a father of vision, teaching them to believe in themselves and to honour their heritage.

This was not the rise of a generation — it was the return of a people.

Miracles in Motion

As the movement grew, miracles began to unfold — not the kind that make headlines, but the kind that change lives.
A school rebuilt by community hands.
A sports team sponsored by local businesses.
A cultural festival revived after decades of silence.

These were signs of rebirth — miracles born from unity and belief.
South Africans began to realise: we are not waiting for change — we are the change.

And as they worked together, hope became visible again.

The Enemies of Rebirth

Of course, not everyone celebrated this awakening.
The moment light rises, shadows react.
Enemies of unity tried to divide.
Fake stories surfaced, twisting truth, painting the Patriot as the problem.
But Gayton did not falter.

He understood that criticism is confirmation — confirmation that something divine was taking shape.
He faced lies with laughter, betrayal with boldness, and fear with faith.

A true patriot does not bend under pressure — he becomes stronger through it.

The Prophetic Alignment

And through every trial, one truth remained clear:
this rebirth was not political — it was prophetic.
It was not man's plan — it was God's alignment.

South Africa, the rainbow nation, had forgotten its colours were meant to blend, not to bleed.
Now, through the alignment of the hearts, the true meaning of unity began to rise again.

The people were rediscovering that love for the land must come with love for each other.
That is the rebirth the ancestors longed for.
That is the dream heaven whispered long ago.

Closing Reflection

Rebirth is not an event — it is a journey.
   It begins when people remember who they are, and it continues when they choose to walk together.

The Coloured Nation, the Khoisan descendants, the youth, and the faithful — all are part of this divine story.
   Through their alignment, the true heart of South Africa beats again.

And as it beats, the world watches in wonder —
   for a people once forgotten have become the builders of a nation reborn.

Chapter 7 — The Rise of the True Patriot

"True patriots are not born in comfort — they are forged in struggle."

From Pain to Purpose

Every great leader is first a story of redemption.

Before Gayton McKenzie became a minister, a movement-builder, or a man of vision, he was a man who had wrestled with the shadows of his own past.

He knew the streets, the hunger, the rejection, and the feeling of being counted out.

He had seen the coldness of cells and the cruelty of systems.

But more importantly, he had seen the mercy of God.

That mercy became the turning point — the divine spark that turned pain into purpose.

He once said,

"My mistakes were my teachers, but grace was my graduation."

From that moment, Gayton stopped living for survival and started living for significance.

He became determined to turn every scar into a source of strength, not for himself, but for his people.

The Transformation

The rise of a true patriot does not begin in boardrooms or campaigns — it begins in the heart.

Gayton's heart was transformed by a personal encounter with God.

He realised that the greatest prison is not made of walls, but of unbelief.

Once faith entered, freedom followed.

He began to read, learn, and rebuild his life.

What society called "a lost cause," God called "a chosen vessel."

And that vessel began to overflow with vision — a vision of restoration, empowerment, and unity.

He used his voice not to boast of power, but to awaken potential.

He became proof that redemption is possible, that grace can rebuild greatness, and that anyone can rise when they choose to align their heart with God's plan.

The Calling of a Patriot

True patriotism does not come from ambition — it comes from calling.

When God places a burden for a nation on a person's heart, no obstacle can silence it.

Gayton's calling was clear: to awaken a sleeping nation, to unite the divided, and to remind the forgotten that they are chosen.

He saw the pain of the Coloured communities, the hopelessness of the youth, and the disunity among races — and he refused to remain silent.

He carried his people's pain in his chest like a heartbeat.
He said,

"I am one of you. I come from where you come from. And together, we will go where God destined us to be."

That is the heart of a true patriot — not to rule over, but to rise with.

A Leader of Action

Leadership, for Gayton, was never about titles.
It was about tangible change.
When he became the Minister of Sport, Arts, and Culture, he didn't start by making speeches — he started by making moves.

He went where others wouldn't go — into forgotten villages, neglected townships, and broken institutions.
He spoke directly to the people, not through filters, but through fellowship.
He listened to athletes who had given up, to artists who had lost hope, to communities who had been left behind.

And then he acted.
He unlocked funding that had sat untouched.
He rebuilt facilities that had crumbled.
He reignited festivals, tournaments, and heritage programs that gave people back their pride.

It wasn't just politics — it was purpose in motion.

Under his leadership, ordinary citizens began to believe again in their worth and in their country.

The Cost of Conviction

But every true patriot must face the test of endurance.

The moment one stands for truth, opposition appears.

As Gayton's influence grew, so did the attacks.

Headlines twisted his story.

Enemies mocked his faith.

Critics tried to paint him as arrogant, divisive, or dangerous.

But through it all, he never wavered.

He often said,

"If they could not break me in darkness, they cannot move me in light."

He knew that the higher one rises, the louder the resistance becomes.

Yet, his strength was not from pride — it was from prayer.

He fought battles on his knees before he fought them in the public square.

Because a true patriot does not fight against his nation — he fights for its soul.

Faith in the Fire

There were days when even his supporters doubted.

Days when promises delayed felt like defeat.

Days when betrayal came from those once trusted.

But Gayton remained unmoved, anchored by faith.

He understood that leadership is not measured by applause but by endurance.

He often reflected on the story of David — a shepherd anointed to be king, but tested in caves before he reached the throne.

Like David, Gayton learned that before you can lead a nation, you must first conquer yourself.

His faith became his fortress.

And through that faith, he learned the secret of true leadership:

"Serve first. Lead second. Love always."

The Rejection That Refined Him

Rejection is a strange gift — it either breaks you or builds you.

For Gayton, it built him.

Every "no" from the world became a "yes" from heaven.

Every attack became a reminder that his mission was not human-made.

He understood that when God calls a man, the world often misunderstands him.

But the same world that mocks you in the beginning, will one day quote you in the end.

He used every insult as fuel, every betrayal as wisdom, every challenge as confirmation.

That is how true patriots rise — not by comfort, but by conviction.

The Alignment of the Hearts

Through his rise, something began to happen across the nation — hearts began to align.

People from all walks of life, of all races and regions, began to see themselves in his story.

They saw a man who had made mistakes but refused to stay down.

They saw a leader who spoke truth without fear, who loved his people without limits, and who carried the dream of South Africa in his soul.

This alignment was not political — it was spiritual.

It was the heartbeat of a reborn nation.

The people began to realise:

"If he can rise, so can we."

And in that realisation, a miracle was born — hope.

The Mark of a True Patriot

Gayton McKenzie's rise was not about power, but about purpose fulfilled.

He didn't just rise as a man — he rose as a message.

He became living proof that God can use anyone to rebuild a nation.

A true patriot is not perfect, but he is purposeful.

He does not seek wealth, but worth.

He does not chase fame, but faithfulness.

He does not rule by fear, but by fervent love.

Through his life, South Africans saw that patriotism is not about politics

— it's about people, principles, and prayer.

Closing Reflection

The rise of Gayton McKenzie is not just the story of one man — it is the story of every South African who refuses to give up.
   It is the echo of a divine truth: that destiny can never be denied when it is aligned with God's plan.

He rose so that others might believe again.
   He stood tall so that others might find courage again.
   He became the voice of a generation rediscovering its identity.

This is the rise of the true patriot —
   a man chosen not by man, but by purpose.
   A man aligned with heaven to heal the heart of a nation.

Chapter 8 — The Heart of Leadership

" Leadership is not about position — it's about permission. The people must give you their hearts before you can lead their hands."

The Calling to Lead

Leadership, in its truest form, is not something a person chases — it is something that chooses them.

When God calls a leader, He does not look at their résumé; He looks at their heart.

Gayton McKenzie's leadership journey did not begin behind a desk or inside a party office.

It began long before that — in broken places, in humble beginnings, in moments when no one believed in him but God.

He learned that before you can lead others, you must first lead yourself.

That meant mastering anger, forgiving betrayal, and walking with humility even when misunderstood.

It meant learning to serve before speaking, to listen before leading, and to pray before planning.

Gayton's leadership was birthed in silence, sharpened in struggle, and revealed in service.

The Servant Before the Leader

When people think of leadership, they often imagine control.
    But Gayton understood a higher truth — to lead is to serve.

He often reminded his team:

"If your people must bow to you, you are not a leader — you are a ruler. But if you kneel to wash their feet, then you are a true servant of the nation."

He visited communities not with arrogance but with compassion.
    He didn't arrive with cameras — he arrived with conversation.
    He sat with the unemployed, the street vendors, the single mothers, the forgotten youth.
    He didn't promise miracles; he offered movement.

Because for him, leadership was not about talking — it was about touching lives.

That humility became his greatest weapon.
    While others built empires, he built relationships.
    While others chased followers, he built family among his people.

Vision Anchored in Values

Every great leader must have a vision, but vision without values is dangerous.

Gayton's vision for South Africa was not born from ego — it was rooted in love and guided by divine principles.

His three pillars of leadership were simple yet powerful:

Integrity — "Do right even when no one sees."

Accountability — "Answer to the people before expecting them to follow."

Compassion — "You can't heal a nation you don't love."

He often said,

"If your vision doesn't serve the people, it's not a vision — it's ambition."

And that's what set him apart.

He didn't seek to be famous; he sought to be faithful.

He didn't want to sit in the highest seat; he wanted to carry the heaviest load.

Leading Through Storms

Every true leader faces storms — not to destroy them, but to define them.

Gayton's storms came in many forms: betrayal, criticism, political sabotage, and moments of deep personal pain.

But each storm only strengthened his foundation.

He learned to trust God more than applause, and purpose more than popularity.

He became unshakable because his leadership was not built on emotion — it was built on conviction.

He often said to his team,

"If your leadership only works when it's easy, you are not leading — you are enjoying comfort. Real leadership begins when it costs you something."

And indeed, it cost him.

It cost friendships, peace, and sometimes even rest.

But he understood that destiny always demands sacrifice.

Raising Leaders, Not Followers

One of Gayton's greatest strengths was that he never wanted to be the only voice.

He believed that a true leader multiplies himself in others.

He mentored young men and women from disadvantaged backgrounds, teaching them not just how to lead, but how to believe.

He saw leadership potential where others saw failure.

He told them,

"You are not too young, too poor, or too broken to lead — you just need to find your why."

He built a culture of empowerment.

He celebrated the success of others without jealousy.

He didn't fear being outshined — he wanted to see others rise even higher.

Because he knew that one leader can start a movement, but many leaders can sustain a nation.

The Burden and the Blessing

Leadership is a heavy crown — not made of gold, but of responsibility.

Gayton carried that crown with grace.

He understood that every decision he made would affect lives, families, and futures.

He spent long nights praying for wisdom, asking God to guide his steps and purify his motives.

He knew that leading a nation's people meant leading its heart.

And the heart of a nation is fragile — it must be handled with truth, justice, and mercy.

He would often say:

"When you lead with love, even correction becomes healing."

And that became his secret — he led not from the throne, but from the heart.

Leadership Through Example

Gayton's power was not in speeches alone — it was in example.

He practiced what he preached.

When he called for transparency, he opened his own books.

When he spoke of unity, he embraced those who once opposed him.

When he urged the youth to rise, he funded their dreams and gave them platforms.

People followed not because of fear, but because of faith in what he stood for.

They saw consistency.

They saw integrity.

They saw a man whose words matched his walk.

That is what makes leadership timeless — when your actions preach louder than your voice.

The Leader Who Listened

In every crowd, Gayton would stop and ask ordinary people what they thought.

He believed wisdom was not reserved for the educated or the elite — it lived in the streets, in the voices of mothers, workers, and youth.

He was not afraid to be corrected.

He understood that listening is the language of respect.

Many who came to challenge him left transformed — not because he argued better, but because he listened deeper.

He said,

"When you listen to people's pain, you earn the right to lead their progress."

That was the heart of his leadership — empathy.

The Power of Love in Leadership

Above all, what made Gayton's leadership different was love.

Not the soft kind that avoids truth — but the strong kind that fights for it.

He loved his people enough to confront corruption, to expose injustice, and to demand excellence.

He loved his country enough to sacrifice his comfort.

His love wasn't emotional — it was actionable.

It looked like feeding the hungry, funding the arts, fixing schools, rebuilding trust.

He believed that leadership without love is tyranny, but love in leadership brings transformation.

He often ended his speeches with one line:

"Let us love our country loudly — not just with words, but with works."

Closing Reflection

The heart of leadership is not found in titles or applause — it's found in service, humility, and love.

Gayton McKenzie's leadership legacy is not just political — it's spiritual.

He reminds us that true leaders are not remembered for how high they stood, but for how deeply they served.

His life is a message to every dreamer, every young patriot, every voice that still believes in a better tomorrow:

"You too can lead — not because you are perfect, but because you are willing."

55

And that is the essence of it all —
    Leadership with a heart.
    Leadership that listens, loves, and lifts.
    Leadership that reflects the very heart of God.

Chapter 9 — The Uniting Spirit of a Nation

"When hearts align, flags rise. When a people remember who they are, a nation is reborn."

A Divided Land in Need of Healing

For generations, South Africa carried the scars of division — scars cut by colour, class, and culture.

Even after freedom came, unity remained fragile. The rainbow seemed faded, the dream delayed.

Communities that once fought side by side began to drift apart again — by politics, by poverty, by pain.

The coloured child felt forgotten,
The black child still waited for fairness,
The white child wrestled with guilt,
And the nation as a whole wrestled with identity.

It was as if the heart of South Africa was beating out of rhythm — longing for healing, longing for truth.

But every generation produces a voice that dares to heal where others only debate.

A voice that calls people not to blame, but to belong.

And in this time, that voice rose — clear, bold, and deeply rooted in love for the people.

That voice was Gayton McKenzie.

The Return of the Spirit of Ubuntu

"Ubuntu" — I am because we are.

Those four words hold the secret to South Africa's soul.

Gayton understood that no policy or speech could heal the country without reviving that spirit.

He began to speak not just to the mind of the nation, but to its heart.

In schools, he told children:

"You are not less. You are the future."

In churches, he reminded pastors:

"The pulpit must speak for the people again."

In townships, he told communities:

"You are the heartbeat of this country — without you, there is no South Africa."

Slowly, something began to shift.

Where there was resentment, there came recognition.

Where there was silence, people began to sing again.

The nation was remembering its own soul.

The Power of Representation

For too long, the Coloured Nation had been told they were "in between."
Too black to be white, too white to be black — too mixed to matter.

Gayton turned that lie into light.
He said,

"We are not in between — we are the bridge!"

That message struck deep across communities.
He gave pride back to the people who had been invisible in their own country.
He told the Coloured youth that they were not leftovers of history, but the living DNA of the rainbow nation.

His leadership made people of every background see themselves not as competitors, but as collaborators — part of one beautiful, complex family called South Africa.

Bridging the Rivers of Blood

Unity cannot be built on denial.
Gayton never ignored the pain of the past — he confronted it with courage.
He reminded the people that forgiveness is not forgetting; it is freeing.

He said:

"We cannot change history, but we can choose not to repeat it. The same blood that once divided us now flows in all of us."

And indeed, in the veins of South Africans runs a tapestry of heritage — Khoisan, Bantu, Malay, Indian, European — all woven by the hand of destiny.

What was once a wound became a witness: proof that God can turn suffering into strength.

Gayton's message was simple — We are one nation with many names, but one destiny.

That truth began to echo through the land like a new national anthem — sung not with instruments, but with hearts.

From Division to Alignment

True alignment happens when purpose overcomes pride.

It is when people stop asking, "Who is right?" and start asking, "What is right for our country?"

Under Gayton's guidance, communities that had once stood apart began to work together — rebuilding schools, feeding the hungry, supporting local artists, and investing in the youth.

Sport, art, and culture became bridges again — tools of healing instead of competition.

He reminded South Africans that unity is not built in parliament halls, but in streets, churches, and homes.

"Unity is not a speech," he said. "It's a lifestyle."

People began to live differently — less divided by language and lineage, more connected by love and legacy.

The Cultural Awakening

As Minister of Sport, Arts, and Culture, Gayton unleashed a cultural revival.

He reopened forgotten museums, funded local artists, supported heritage projects, and told the stories no one had told — the stories of the Coloured heroes, Khoisan kings, and unsung women of courage who shaped South Africa's soul.

He reminded the youth that culture is not just clothing or dance — it is identity.

He pushed for local films, music, and poetry that reflected the people themselves.

The nation began to see that being South African is not about fitting into a mould — it's about celebrating our differences as divine design.

When Love Becomes Law

What began as a movement became a moral awakening.

Gayton's leadership was no longer about a party — it was about a people.

He reminded the nation that love is the highest law of leadership.

"You can't build a nation you don't love, and you can't love a people you don't know."

By learning about one another — our languages, our foods, our histories

— South Africans began to rediscover themselves.

The barriers of colour started to fall, replaced by the bridges of compassion.

The once divided hearts began to align.

The Spirit of a New South Africa

Across townships and cities, across provinces and parties, a new spirit began to stir.

It wasn't the spirit of politics — it was the spirit of patriotism.

It was the sound of a people waking up to their divine destiny.

A nation once broken was now believing again.

Believing in hope.

Believing in unity.

Believing in itself.

The world began to notice: a miracle was happening in South Africa — not through laws or leaders alone, but through the alignment of hearts.

Closing Reflection

The uniting spirit of a nation does not come through force — it comes through forgiveness.

It comes when people remember that their shared pain is smaller than their shared purpose.

Under the heart of a true patriot, South Africa found its reflection again — not in division, but in destiny.

Not in skin, but in soul.

Not in history, but in healing.

And so the prophecy began to unfold —
    The first people's children were standing again.
    A nation once divided was learning to dance together again.
    And the heart of Africa was beating in one rhythm:
    Ubuntu. Unity. Love. Alignment.

Chapter 10 — Miracles in Motion

"When a leader's heart aligns with heaven, miracles begin to move through the hands of the people."

A New Dawn

When Gayton McKenzie stepped into the office of the Minister of Sport, Arts and Culture, he did not come as a politician — he came as a patriot with purpose.

He walked into his new role not with pride, but with prayer.

He told his staff,

"We are not here to manage — we are here to minister."

That was the difference.

He saw his department not as a building of bureaucracy, but as a bridge of blessing.

From his very first day, he carried a clear message:

"We will restore what was broken, revive what was forgotten, and reward what is good."

And from that declaration, the miracles began.

The Miracle of Restoration

The first miracle wasn't in money — it was in mindset.

He brought dignity back to artists, athletes, and cultural workers who had been forgotten by the system.

He reopened abandoned community centres and turned them into creative hubs.

He launched "Sport for All" programs that reached even the smallest towns, ensuring children in dusty fields could dream again.

He funded art schools, revived cultural festivals, and restored the pride of communities who had felt invisible.

"The artist," he said, "is not a luxury — they are the lungs of the nation."

He made sure forgotten sports like boxing, netball, and indigenous games received equal honour.

He invested in museums telling the true story of South Africa's roots — from Khoisan heritage to modern music legends.

Everywhere he went, the message was clear:

South Africa belongs to all who live in it — and every gift deserves a stage.

The Miracle of Accountability

Miracles are not magic — they are the fruit of discipline.

Gayton knew that corruption was the silent killer of progress.

He refused to allow waste or dishonesty in his ministry.

He opened the books.

He audited every contract.

He cancelled wasteful projects that enriched a few and redirected funds to empower many.

His leadership brought something people had long lost — trust.

He told his team,

"Transparency is not an option; it's our testimony."

The newspapers that once attacked him were forced to report the results:
schools being built, artists being paid, athletes being sponsored, communities being served.
The people began to say,

"We finally have a minister who works like a patriot."

And that was a miracle — not of politics, but of principle.

The Miracle of Opportunity

Under his vision, the doors of opportunity opened wider than ever before.
Young creatives were given grants and mentorships.
Rural athletes received equipment and transport to national events.
Cultural groups once ignored were invited to national showcases.

He built programs that didn't just help people — they activated them.
He believed every person carried a gift, and that the government's job was not to replace their efforts but to release their potential.

He told the youth,

"We don't want you to wait for help — we want you to become the help."

And they did.

Communities that once felt powerless began to produce champions, filmmakers, painters, and leaders.

The miracle wasn't just happening to them — it was happening through them.

The Miracle of Unity Through Culture

Gayton used art and sport as divine instruments of unity.

He believed that where politicians argue, music heals.

Where policies divide, sport unites.

He launched the "One Nation Cup" — a national sports event where teams from every background, race, and province competed not as rivals, but as brothers and sisters.

He revived the national arts week under a new theme: "From Diversity to Destiny."

Suddenly, the language of unity was not spoken only in speeches — it was sung, painted, and played.

People began to see their neighbour not as an opponent, but as a partner in destiny.

It was as if South Africa's heartbeat began to synchronize again — one rhythm, one purpose, one spirit.

The Miracle of the Arts

Under his leadership, South Africa's artists began to flourish.

He made sure the creative industry received the respect it deserved — fair pay, recognition, and opportunity.

Local theatres filled up again.
Traditional dances returned to national festivals.
Films made in townships began winning international awards.

He told filmmakers:

"Tell our stories — the world needs to hear them."

He believed that art is prophecy — the ability to show people who they are and who they can become.
Through his policies, art became not only entertainment, but education.

The youth began to see creativity as a career, not a hobby.
The nation began to remember that culture is not what separates us — it's what connects us.

The Miracle of Forgiveness

While his success was growing, so were the attacks.
False headlines, political jealousy, and twisted narratives tried to discredit him.
But Gayton never fought with hate.
He answered with humility.

"If I must be misunderstood to serve my people, then let me be misunderstood," he said.

He forgave those who mocked him.
    He refused to respond with bitterness.
    He kept his eyes on the mission, not the noise.

And in that silence, people saw the truth.
    The more they attacked, the more his work spoke for itself.
    Because no rumour can erase real results.

The Miracle of Rebirth

The ministry began to feel alive — vibrant, energetic, purpose-driven.
    Civil servants became servants of the people again.
    Communities once ignored became centres of innovation.
    Artists who once begged for support became ambassadors of hope.

It was more than reform — it was revival.
    People said, "We've never seen this before."
    And indeed, they hadn't.

Because what they were witnessing was not politics — it was prophecy.
    The prophecy that the children of the first people would rise again to
restore balance and beauty in the land.
    And they did — under the leadership of a man whose heart was aligned
with heaven.

Closing Reflection

Miracles don't always look like lightning — sometimes they look like
leadership.
    They look like schools reopened, artists empowered, youth inspired,
and families united.

They look like a nation remembering its worth.

Gayton McKenzie didn't wait for miracles — he became one.

His story reminds us that when the heart of a true patriot beats for his people, God moves through that heartbeat.

For the first time in a long time, South Africa wasn't just surviving —

it was shining.

And the world began to see what happens when a nation aligns its heart with purpose:

Miracles move.

Chapter 11 — The Battle for the Soul of the Nation

"Every time light begins to rise, darkness grows restless."

When the Enemy Notices Progress

Every movement of truth will always awaken a reaction.

When the works of Gayton McKenzie began to bear fruit — when schools reopened, when athletes triumphed, when forgotten communities stood proud again — not everyone rejoiced.

The forces that had fed on division, corruption, and chaos suddenly felt threatened.

Old systems that survived by keeping people silent began to tremble.

They could not stand a leader who refused to be bought or broken.

And so the battle began — not with guns and soldiers, but with words, whispers, and lies.

Newspapers twisted stories.

Political rivals launched smear campaigns.

Social media buzzed with false accusations.

But while others shouted, Gayton remained silent.

He knew that every great calling comes with great opposition.

He told his team,

"If the enemy fights this hard, it's because he fears what God is about to do."

The Unseen War

This was not merely a political fight — it was spiritual warfare.

The destiny of a nation was being contested in unseen realms.

For South Africa was not just battling for progress — it was battling for its soul.

The spirit of greed, corruption, and racial hatred had long enslaved the land.

Every leader who tried to break it was attacked, discredited, or destroyed.

But this time, something was different.

This time, a movement was led not by ambition, but by alignment.

Gayton stood not with arrogance, but with authority from above.

He said,

"You can destroy my image, but you cannot destroy my impact. I stand for something greater than myself."

The storm was fierce, but his faith was fierce too.

Because he understood:

The purpose of the storm is to test the strength of your foundation.

Attacks and Accusations

Headlines filled the air —
   "Scandal!"
   "Controversy!"
   "Corruption!"

But every accusation crumbled under truth.
   Investigations found nothing but integrity and action.
   The people saw it clearly — the attack was not on Gayton alone, but on the hope he represented.

Still, the blows hurt.
   Even strong men bleed.
   He faced betrayal from those he trusted, and pressure from those who feared his rise.
   But he didn't retreat; he regrouped.

He reminded his followers:

"We do not fight flesh and blood, but spirits and systems. Our weapon is not revenge — it is righteousness."

And that truth began to empower others.
   People prayed again.
   Communities stood behind him.
   A movement that had started with one heart began to move as one army.

The Testing of Faith

In quiet moments, Gayton often prayed alone.

He didn't ask God for protection — he asked for perseverance.

He knew that to carry a nation's destiny, he had to first carry its pain.

He opened his Bible and read:

"No weapon formed against you shall prosper." (Isaiah 54:17)

Those words became his daily strength.

He understood that leadership is not about avoiding trials, but enduring them.

Because the higher the calling, the heavier the cross.

He was not just leading a political cause — he was leading a spiritual awakening.

And such awakenings are always born through warfare.

The Spirit of Division Returns

The enemy's oldest weapon is division.

He tried to turn communities against one another — black against coloured, rich against poor, north against south.

Social media became a battlefield of words and rumours.

But Gayton countered not with anger, but with truth.

He reminded South Africans that the real fight was not among themselves, but against the systems that wanted them divided.

"We are one people," he declared, "and if we stay divided, we stay defeated."

He began launching reconciliation events — bringing together leaders from different backgrounds to pray, talk, and plan for peace.

He used sport as a platform to promote unity, and art as a language of love.

Slowly, the fires of division began to fade again — replaced by the light of brotherhood.

The Silence that Speaks

Sometimes, Gayton chose silence instead of defending himself.

He knew that in a world full of noise, silence can be the loudest sermon.

He let his actions answer his accusers.

He let his work speak when words failed.

Every project completed, every youth program launched, every family helped — each became a living testimony that truth cannot be buried.

The people began to see through the noise.

They said, "We know his heart — and no lie can change that."

The media's grip began to weaken because you cannot drown a voice that carries purpose.

The People Rise

It was then that something extraordinary happened — the people themselves began to rise.

Communities started defending his name publicly.

Artists, athletes, and ordinary citizens began speaking up.

They said:

"He stands for us — and we will stand for him."

It was not blind loyalty.
    It was gratitude.
    They had seen real change, and they refused to let darkness undo it.

The movement was no longer about one man — it was about a mission.
    The mission to protect the soul of South Africa.
    To prove that integrity still exists.
    To remind the world that one heart aligned with God can shift an entire nation.

The Victory of Character

Eventually, the truth always outlives the lie.
    The storms passed, the noise faded, and what remained was the fruit.
    Sports continued to thrive.
    Artists continued to rise.
    Communities continued to be transformed.

Those who once mocked were now silent.
    Because character always wins where cleverness fails.

Gayton's life became living proof that real victory is not in defeating enemies, but in remaining faithful to your calling.
    He didn't need revenge — he had results.
    He didn't need to justify — he just kept working.

And in that consistency, the people saw the mark of a true patriot:
    A man who doesn't quit when it hurts, but keeps going because it's right.

Closing Reflection

The battle for the soul of a nation is not fought with guns or slogans —
it's fought with truth, faith, and endurance.
    Every patriot must understand: opposition is the evidence of impact.
    If darkness fights you, it's because your light is too bright to ignore.

South Africa's destiny was being written through the struggle — not to
destroy her, but to define her.
    And through it all, one heart remained unbroken, one vision stayed
alive, one leader kept believing that the dream of unity was worth every
wound.

Because in the end, patriotism is not proven in peace — it is proven in
battle.
    And Gayton McKenzie stood, battered but unbent,
    A soldier of light,
    A servant of truth,
    A true patriot whose heart never left the people.

Chapter 12 — The Rebirth of Hope

"After every winter, the soil remembers how to bloom."

A New Dawn

The sun rose over South Africa, and it felt different.
The air carried a stillness — a sacred calm after the storm.
The noise of politics began to fade, replaced by the sound of rebuilding.

Communities that once stood divided began working side by side.
From the Cape Flats to Soweto, from Gqeberha to Kimberly — something new was stirring.
A quiet revolution — not of anger, but of alignment.

The seeds Gayton McKenzie and the Patriotic Alliance had planted in faith were now breaking through the soil of despair.
It was not just a political victory — it was spiritual renewal.

South Africa was remembering who she truly was.
Not a country cursed by its past, but a nation chosen for greatness.

The Return of the Forgotten

For years, coloured communities had felt invisible — trapped between history and hope.

But under Gayton's leadership, the forgotten found their voice again.

He said:

"You were not created to be in-between. You were created to be a bridge."

That truth hit deep.

It was not just a statement — it was healing.

Young men who had lost faith in politics began volunteering at community centres.

Mothers who once stood in welfare lines began starting small businesses.

The spirit of dependency was being replaced by dignity.

The message was clear: No one is coming to save us — we are the ones we've been waiting for.

Miracles in Motion

As Minister of Sport, Arts and Culture, Gayton McKenzie launched projects that transformed lives.

Sports fields were rebuilt in townships that had been abandoned for decades.

Art schools reopened.

Youth festivals returned.

Children from poor backgrounds now competed internationally — not as victims, but as victors.

A soccer player from Eldorado Park became a national hero.

A poet from Mitchells Plain stood on a world stage.

A painter from Kimberley sold art to European galleries.

The ripple effect was breathtaking.

The nation was reminded: talent is everywhere, it just needs opportunity.

Gayton made sure opportunity was no longer reserved for the privileged few — it belonged to every South African.

The Spirit of Ubuntu Returns

Ubuntu — "I am because we are."

These were more than words; they became a lifestyle again.

The divisions that apartheid had carved deep into the soul of the nation began to heal through acts of kindness.

People started helping one another again — not because of race or politics, but because they were human.

Churches, schools, NGOs, and even rival movements began partnering for one purpose: the restoration of South Africa.

Sport became the new pulpit of unity.

Art became the language of reconciliation.

And music — once used to protest — now became the sound of celebration.

A Nation Rediscovers Its Soul

Gayton travelled across the provinces, speaking not as a politician, but as a father figure.

He didn't come with big words — he came with heart.

He told stories of his past, of prison, of pain, and of purpose.

And people connected, because they saw themselves in him.

He told them:

"I am not perfect, but I am proof that change is possible."

Crowds cried, cheered, and prayed together.

He didn't speak to them — he spoke for them.

He carried the heartbeat of the streets, the rhythm of the working class, the pride of the coloured, the resilience of the black, and the hope of the white.

It was no longer his story — it was ours.

The Power of Restoration

The same media that once attacked him now began to report the impact.

Numbers didn't lie — crime rates dropped around community sports hubs.

Young artists were earning incomes through government-supported programs.

International investors started to notice the new energy in the country's creative sector.

Even skeptics had to admit — something real was happening.

He had done in months what others couldn't do in decades — not because of money or politics, but because of heart.

"When you love your people, they respond," he said.
"When you serve with honesty, they follow."

And that became the secret of his success — servant leadership.

The Alignment of Prophecy

Prophets and intercessors across South Africa began to speak of what they saw — a shift in the spirit.
They said:

"God is raising leaders with clean hands and burning hearts."

Gayton's journey was no longer just political — it was prophetic.
Many began to see his rise as part of a divine pattern — the fulfilment of words spoken long ago about a man from among the people who would restore dignity to the land.

He didn't claim to be that man — but his life carried the signs.
The timing.
The trials.
The transformation.

All aligned perfectly with what God had promised over the rainbow nation — that South Africa would become a light to the world.

Healing Through Heritage

As Minister, Gayton made heritage a living thing again.
He launched programs to preserve the stories of unsung heroes — fishermen, miners, single mothers, street musicians, teachers, and

community builders.

He said,

"Every South African has a story worth remembering."

Museums became storytelling hubs.

Heritage Day became more than a public holiday — it became a national day of gratitude.

Through arts, culture, and history, South Africans began to heal from the pain of the past.

Because only by honouring your roots can you grow new branches.

The Rebirth of Faith

Churches began to overflow again — not out of fear, but out of renewed faith.

People prayed for their leaders.

Pastors spoke of hope instead of hopelessness.

The gospel and the government began working side by side — feeding the hungry, uplifting the youth, and bringing peace into broken homes.

The wall between church and state became a bridge.

Faith was no longer just preached — it was practiced.

This was the rebirth of hope — not man-made, but God-breathed.

Closing Reflection

Hope had returned to the land — not as a speech, not as a slogan, but as a spirit.

The people began to believe again.

Children dreamed again.

The anthem sounded different again.

For the first time in a long time, the nation could look itself in the mirror and say,

"We are healing. We are rising. We are one."

And at the centre of it all stood a man — flawed, but faithful — who never gave up on his people, because his heart had aligned with the heartbeat of God for South Africa.

He was more than a minister.

He was more than a politician.

He was a true patriot.

The story was far from over — but the light was now unstoppable.

Chapter 13 — A Movement Becomes a Nation

"When hearts align, flags no longer divide — they unite."

The Birth of a Movement

It started with conversations in small rooms, with people who simply wanted better for their communities.

No fancy offices, no media teams, no sponsors — just vision.

The Patriotic Alliance was born out of pain, purpose, and prayer.

It was never meant to be another political machine; it was a family of believers, dreamers, and doers.

A colourful alliance for a colourful nation.

In the beginning, the world laughed.

"Another party," they said.

"Another promise," they muttered.

But they didn't see the deeper truth — that this was not about politics.

It was about people.

It was about hearts aligning for something greater than power — for purpose.

The Voice of the Voiceless

As the Alliance grew, something miraculous happened.

Ordinary South Africans — people who had given up on hope — began to speak again.

A teacher in Upington started a reading club for children.

A fisherman in Saldanha started mentoring boys to keep them off drugs.

A nurse in Mitchells Plain began a feeding scheme for families.

These weren't government projects.

They were Patriot projects.

Self-started. Self-driven.

People taking ownership of their country again.

They realized they didn't need permission to make a difference — only passion and purpose.

The Message that Moved Mountains

Gayton McKenzie's message was simple but powerful:

"Love your country enough to fix it yourself."

He didn't tell people to wait for miracles — he told them to become miracles.

He reminded them that South Africa's story had always been written by ordinary people who refused to quit.

And that message caught fire.

From Karoo farms to inner-city streets, people began identifying as patriots.

Not because of race or region — but because of heart.

Suddenly, being a patriot wasn't just about politics; it was a lifestyle.

It meant cleaning your community, mentoring youth, honouring elders, supporting local business, protecting women and children, and believing again in your flag.

Unity in Colour

One of the miracles of the movement was its diversity.

In meetings, you'd find Zulu, Xhosa, Sotho, Afrikaner, Coloured, and Indian brothers and sisters sitting side by side — not arguing, but agreeing.

They called it "the Rainbow Table."

At that table, no one was above another.

Everyone's story mattered.

It was the first time many had seen unity that was not forced, but felt.

The coloured people, carrying the blended heritage of the nation, became living symbols of unity — proof that South Africa's bloodlines had already mixed long before politics tried to separate them.

The Koisan history — the first people of the land — began to shine again.

Their legacy of peace, wisdom, and connection to the earth became the heartbeat of the new South African identity.

From Party to Purpose

The Alliance began to evolve.

It was no longer content with winning votes — it wanted to win souls back to hope.

It moved beyond rallies and policies into purposeful living.

It became a nation within a nation — a brotherhood and sisterhood of patriots who carried the same fire in their hearts:

to see South Africa restored to greatness.

From schools to prisons, from churches to sports fields — the movement spread like wildfire.

People who had never spoken politics before were now discussing destiny.

Even those who didn't agree with every policy respected the purpose.

Because purpose speaks louder than politics.

Miracles of Multiplication

The good Gayton started in one province began echoing across others.

Every project birthed another.

Every act of kindness inspired ten more.

A feeding scheme in the Northern Cape inspired one in the Eastern Cape.

A youth soccer league in Eldorado Park inspired one in Durban.

A community art gallery in Beaufort West inspired one in Mamelodi.

The government had started programs before, but this was different — it wasn't funded by money, it was fueled by love.

And that love became unstoppable.

The Spirit of Servant Leadership

The key to this transformation was Gayton's heart.
He didn't stand above his people — he stood among them.
He didn't demand honour — he earned it.

When floods hit KwaZulu-Natal, he was there carrying sandbags.
When children in Northern Cape needed shoes, he helped deliver them.
When artists in Johannesburg felt forgotten, he sat with them — not for cameras, but for compassion.

People began calling him not "Minister," but "Brother Gayton."
Because he embodied what every patriot should be — a servant first, a leader second.

He often said:

"If I eat and my neighbour is hungry, then I am not yet free."

That philosophy became the moral code of the Alliance.

The Alignment of Hearts

The power of the Patriotic Alliance was never in its structure — it was in its spirit.
It was born from alignment — spiritual, emotional, and national.
People's hearts began to beat in rhythm again.

Black, White, Coloured, Indian — differences didn't disappear, but they no longer divided.
They became threads in one flag, woven together by shared destiny.

The rebirth of South Africa wasn't coming from Parliament — it was coming from people.

From those who had been overlooked, underestimated, and underestimated — rising up in unity and saying,

"We are the nation we've been praying for."

The Call Beyond Borders

Soon, other African nations began to take notice.

Leaders from Namibia, Botswana, Zimbabwe, and even across the ocean started asking,

"What is happening in South Africa?"

They saw communities thriving without waiting for government aid.

They saw young people leading with hope instead of hate.

They saw revival — political, cultural, and spiritual.

And they realized — the fire of patriotism is contagious.

The true patriot does not fight only for his nation, but for humanity.

Gayton's message became Africa's echo:

"Be proud of who you are. Be united. Be unstoppable."

Closing Reflection

What began as a movement became a miracle.

A family became a nation.

A party became a purpose.

This was no longer about one man, one city, or one colour — it was about a destiny unfolding before the eyes of the world.

And in that destiny, South Africa began to remember the truth it had forgotten for too long:

"We are not enemies. We are one people, under one God, standing on one sacred land."

The fire of patriotism had ignited, and it would not be put out again.

The True Patriot was no longer a title — it was an identity.
A way of life.
A call to action.
A rebirth of the rainbow nation's soul.

Chapter 14 — The Fire Within the Youth

A group of young men in Eldorado Park started a free soccer league for kids.

A group of girls in Gqeberha created a mobile art studio to paint murals of hope in drug-infested areas.

A Cape Town rapper wrote a hit song titled "Aligned Hearts," that became the anthem of the new youth movement.

Chapter 15 — The Arts of Alignment

"When words fail, art speaks the truth of the heart."

The Language of the Soul

Every nation has a sound — a rhythm that defines its soul. For South Africa, that sound had always been rich and colourful: the beat of drums, the melody of choirs, the laughter of street musicians, the rhythm of township poetry.

But for years, the arts had been starved.

Artists struggled.

Musicians begged for funding.

Poets spoke to empty rooms.

The creative flame that once united the nation had dimmed under neglect and poverty.

Then came a turning point — a man with vision, a leader with a listening ear.

When Gayton McKenzie became the Minister of Sport, Arts, and Culture, the arts of the nation began to breathe again.

The Revival of the Stage

Gayton understood that sport builds strength, but art builds spirit.
   He declared,

"A nation without art is a nation without voice."

His ministry began restoring community theatres, sponsoring cultural festivals, and reopening art schools that had been forgotten.
   Theatre groups returned to town halls.
   Musicians got grants to record albums.
   Film crews began shooting local stories again — South African stories.

Every province began to showcase its own identity — proudly, loudly, and beautifully.
   The arts were no longer a luxury — they became a ministry of unity.

The Sound of a New South Africa

Music became the messenger of the rebirth.
   Radio stations began playing more local songs.
   Amapiano, gospel, hip-hop, and jazz artists started collaborating across cultural lines.
   Lyrics began to carry a different tone — not of anger or despair, but of hope and healing.

One hit song, "We Are One Blood," written by young artists from Cape Town, Pretoria, and Durban, topped charts for months.
   The chorus said:

"We've been broken, we've been bruised,

But we rise with the same blood in our veins —
The blood of Africa, the song of the brave."

It became the anthem of the movement — a reminder that South Africa's true strength was not in politics, but in people.

Poetry of the Patriots

Poets began to rise again, carrying truth on their tongues.
   At youth events, church gatherings, and public festivals, they spoke fire — words that healed, words that united.

A young poet from the Northern Cape performed a piece titled "Aligned Hearts," saying:

"We were scattered, but not lost,
   Divided, but not destroyed.
   The soil still knows our names,
   The wind still carries our songs."

The crowd stood in tears.
   Poetry had become prophecy again.

The arts were not just entertainment — they were education.
   They taught people where they came from, who they were, and what they were destined to become.

Film as a Mirror of Truth

Under Gayton's leadership, local filmmakers received the support they had prayed for.

Stories that had long been silenced finally reached the screen — stories of the Koisan, of township mothers, of unsung heroes, of men who rose from nothing to change everything.

The South African Film Fund launched dozens of community-based projects, allowing small towns to tell their own stories.

Documentaries showed the real faces of patriotism — not celebrities, but ordinary people making extraordinary impact.

International festivals began to notice.

The world saw a new wave of South African cinema — proud, raw, and redemptive.

And through film, the message of the True Patriot began to echo beyond borders.

Dance of the Reborn

Dance became the physical language of unity.

Cultural groups mixed traditional styles with modern moves — Zulu meets jazz, Khoisan steps with Amapiano beats, Tswana rhythms blending with coloured line dancing.

It was history meeting the present in joyful motion.

At national events, people danced not just for fun, but as worship.

Every movement declared:

"We are still here. We are still strong. We are still one."

For many young people, dance became their way out of darkness — a way to express what words could not say.

The ministry began funding township dance academies and school programs, bringing discipline, confidence, and joy back to youth culture.

The Art of Healing

Art heals because it allows truth to breathe.
Gayton often said:

"Let the artists speak. Their words will build where politics has failed."

And they did.
Pain was turned into paintings.
Struggle was turned into songs.
Loss was turned into poems.
And unity was painted on walls from Johannesburg to George.

Mural projects began colouring township walls with hope — giant paintings of South African heroes, scripture verses, and patriotic symbols.
Each wall became a sermon, reminding everyone: We are still alive. We are still chosen.

The Spirit of Collaboration

What made this artistic revival historic was unity.
For the first time, artists worked together across colour and genre lines.
White classical musicians performed with black choirs.
Coloured poets collaborated with Zulu dancers.
Afrikaans songwriters and Xhosa rappers recorded together — and the result was magic.

These collaborations became more than performances — they were prophetic pictures of what South Africa could be: different, yet deeply connected.

A Nation Painted Anew

As arts flourished, so did identity.
   People began to take pride again in their heritage.
   The Koisan people were celebrated as the root of the nation — the heartbeat of the land.
   Cultural museums were updated, telling the truth about South Africa's origins, the pain of colonization, and the beauty of survival.

The story of the Coloured Nation — once silenced — began to shine.
   No longer forgotten, they were recognized as the bridges of the nation — carrying the blood of many tribes, the spirit of all races, and the legacy of resilience.

Gayton's ministry called this initiative "Heritage in Motion."
   It was not about the past — it was about reclaiming identity for the future.

Closing Reflection

Through the arts, South Africa rediscovered her voice.
   Through creativity, she found healing.
   Through culture, she found connection.
   Through expression, she found alignment.

The arts became the heartbeat of patriotism.
   Because when a nation learns to sing again, it learns to love again.

The stage lights of theatres, the colours of murals, the harmony of choirs — all became one anthem:

"We are one people. We are one heart. We are one nation — reborn."

The brush, the drum, and the pen had become sacred instruments of unity.
And as the people created, they began to understand —
Art is the voice of the True Patriot.

Chapter 16 — The Fields of Unity

"On the field, we are not many — we are one flag, one heartbeat, one people."

The Power of the Game

South Africa has always been a land of champions.

From the dusty soccer fields of Soweto to the rugby pitches of Cape Town, from netball courts in rural schools to cricket ovals in small towns — the spirit of competition has always been alive.

But for decades, sport in the nation was broken.

Inequality, poor facilities, lack of funding, and political division had poisoned what was once pure joy.

Many young talents gave up because they had no shoes, no fields, no chance.

Then came a moment of divine timing — a new Minister with a player's heart and a leader's vision.

When Gayton McKenzie took office as Minister of Sport, Arts and Culture, he didn't just talk about change.

He became the change.

Rebuilding the Dream

Gayton knew that to rebuild a nation, you must first rebuild hope.

And where better to start than in the very place where young hearts dream — the sports fields of South Africa.

He began traveling the country, visiting forgotten clubs, old stadiums, and schools with broken nets and faded lines.

He didn't arrive in fancy cars or suits — he arrived as one of them.

He listened. He asked questions.

He promised, and then he delivered.

Old fields were restored.

Communities received sports kits, coaches, and funding.

Partnerships were formed with local businesses to support community teams.

Rural schools were given the same opportunities as private ones.

The message was clear:

"Talent is not born in privilege — it is born in purpose."

The Golden Fields Initiative

One of his first national projects was called The Golden Fields Initiative.

Its mission was simple — to plant new fields of unity across the nation.

From Limpopo to the Western Cape, dozens of community stadiums were built or renovated.

Each one carried the flag of South Africa and a mural of unity — Coloured, Black, White, Indian, and Koisan children hand-in-hand.

Each opening day was celebrated not as a government event, but as a family reunion of the nation.

These fields became sacred ground — places where children learned not only to play, but to belong.
Where enemies became teammates.
Where races became brothers and sisters.

Uniting Through Sport

Under Gayton's leadership, sport became more than competition — it became conversation.

Rugby clubs began visiting soccer teams.
Cricket players helped train netball teams.
Local tournaments became community festivals filled with music, food, and dance.

The nation began to witness a miracle:
People who once argued over politics now stood side by side, cheering for the same local team.
In stadiums, on playgrounds, and even in dusty fields — unity was reborn.

The Return of National Pride

South Africa began winning again — not only trophies, but hearts.
National teams started performing with renewed fire.
Athletes proudly declared their love for the country, saying,

"We play for the people, not the politics."

Gayton attended games not as a distant minister, but as a fan —
shouting, clapping, laughing, standing in the crowd.

He reminded the world that leadership means standing with the
people, not above them.

When South Africa hosted continental and international tournaments,
the nation's hospitality shone.

Foreign players spoke of the love, the music, and the warmth they
felt.

It was no longer just sport — it was a movement of heart.

Empowering the Forgotten

True to his word, Gayton made sure sport reached where it had never
reached before — into the forgotten corners of the land.

Prisons were given sports programs for rehabilitation.

Townships received street soccer leagues.

Women's sports, once ignored, received record-breaking funding.

Disabled athletes were honoured and supported with better training
and visibility.

One young Paralympian from Kimberley said,

"Minister Gayton didn't see my wheelchair — he saw my dream."

That statement echoed through the nation — proof that true patriotism
sees potential, not position.

The Spirit of the Game

Gayton often said:

"The field doesn't care about your surname — it only cares about your heart."

That became the philosophy behind the Fields of Unity Movement.

Teams were encouraged to mentor one another, sharing training sessions across racial and economic divides.

Children learned discipline, teamwork, and faith through sport.

Churches partnered with sports clubs, holding prayer meetings before big games.

Athletes began dedicating victories to their communities, not just to themselves.

The field became a sanctuary — a place of worship through motion.

The Day of Champions

One unforgettable day came when a national youth tournament gathered children from all nine provinces.

Thousands filled a newly rebuilt stadium.

Gayton walked onto the field, surrounded by children holding hands in a circle of every colour and culture.

He said:

"This is what the Kingdom of God looks like — united, joyful, victorious."

And the crowd erupted in song.

The anthem of the movement rang out across the land:

"We play as one. We win as one. We are South Africa — one heart, one home."

It was more than a sports day — it was a prophetic picture of alignment.

From Competition to Compassion

Sport began healing old wounds.
   Rivals started visiting each other's communities.
   Games were played not for glory, but for charity.
   Tournaments raised funds for schools, hospitals, and families in need.

Every event carried a message: Play for a purpose.
   And that purpose was unity.

The Legacy of the Fields

Years later, people began to notice something deeper:
   Crime rates dropped where sports programs were active.
   Children stayed in school.
   Communities stopped fighting and started collaborating.

The fields were no longer just grass and paint — they had become gardens of hope.
   And through them, Gayton McKenzie's vision was coming to life: a South Africa where every person, no matter their background, could find belonging.

Closing Reflection

Sport had done what politics could not — it had aligned hearts.

It had shown that true power is not in control, but in connection.
Every kick, every cheer, every handshake became a prayer for peace.

In every victory and defeat, South Africa learned something sacred:

"The spirit of sport is the spirit of the True Patriot — fair, fearless, faithful."

The fields of unity became the heart of the nation.
And through them, the people rediscovered not only their strength, but their oneness.

Chapter 17 — The Rebuilding of Culture

"A nation without culture is a nation without memory. A nation that forgets its memory, loses its destiny."

The Awakening of Identity

When Gayton McKenzie became the Minister of Sport, Arts and Culture, South Africa was at a crossroads.

The youth were disconnected from their roots.

Many no longer spoke their mother tongues.

Cultural traditions were seen as outdated.

And the stories of the Koisan — the First People of the Land — had been buried under centuries of silence.

But Gayton saw something different.

He saw that to heal the nation, one must first rebuild its identity.

He declared,

"Before we can move forward as a nation, we must remember who we are — and who we were meant to be."

That was the birth of the Cultural Reawakening Movement, a campaign that swept across provinces, reviving pride, honour, and history.

The Return of the Forgotten Stories

Under Gayton's leadership, museums and cultural centres were revived.
Forgotten archives were opened.
The true stories of the Koisan, the Coloured Nation, and all indigenous peoples began to emerge — not as fragments of history, but as foundations of identity.

The ministry partnered with historians, elders, and storytellers to record the oral traditions that had been fading away.
Elders from rural areas were invited to share their knowledge, songs, and ancient customs.

A museum in Upington was dedicated to the history of the Koisan, showcasing their language, tools, art, and spirituality.
In every province, monuments were built to honour those who had been erased from history — the unsung heroes of freedom.

Language — The Soul of Culture

One of Gayton's most powerful initiatives was the Language Revival Project.
He believed that every language carries divine identity — that to silence a language is to silence a people's spirit.

Under this vision, schools began reintroducing indigenous languages like Nama, Xhosa, Tswana, Zulu, Afrikaans, and Khoekhoe as part of their main curriculum.
Children were encouraged to speak their native tongues with pride.

"When a child speaks their mother's language," Gayton said,
"the ancestors smile — because the bloodline remembers."

Television and radio stations were given incentives to broadcast in multiple local languages.

Poetry competitions and cultural festivals celebrated the beauty of expression in every dialect.

South Africans began to fall in love again — with their own voices.

The Rebirth of Traditional Arts

Artisans, crafters, beadworkers, and musicians began receiving recognition and funding.

Cultural markets were opened across towns, showcasing handmade goods and traditional attire.

Every piece of beadwork told a story.

Every song carried history.

Every dance was a testimony of survival.

Communities once ashamed of their traditions began to wear their culture proudly again.

Young people learned the dances of their elders — the Riel, the Ghoema, the Gumboot, the Xibelani.

It became more than movement — it became memory in motion.

The ministry launched the Pride in Heritage Campaign, which encouraged South Africans to wear traditional clothing every Friday.

Soon, government buildings, offices, and schools were filled with colour — a living rainbow of identity.

Celebrating the Koisan Heritage

For centuries, the Koisan people — the first inhabitants of Southern Africa — were treated as invisible.

Their bloodline runs through the veins of millions of South Africans, especially the Coloured community, yet their story had been distorted or erased.

Gayton made it his mission to restore dignity to the First Nation People.

He established cultural recognition programs that acknowledged the Koisan's historical and spiritual importance to the land.

Festivals celebrating Koisan culture — their music, food, and ancient traditions — became national events.

He said,

"They are not forgotten — they are the root.

And a tree without roots cannot stand."

Through this movement, the nation began to understand that unity does not erase difference — it honours it.

The Koisan were no longer seen as relics of the past, but as keepers of sacred knowledge — the heart of the land itself.

Faith and Culture — The Divine Alignment

Gayton often spoke of how God had a divine plan for South Africa.

He believed the rebuilding of culture was not only political or social — it was spiritual.

He said,

"God is aligning this nation again with its original purpose.
    The land that once bled will now bloom.
    The people who were forgotten will now lead."

Churches and cultural leaders began working together — merging faith and heritage.
    Ceremonies of thanksgiving were held in open fields, where prayers were lifted in every language.
    Pastors, imams, and traditional leaders stood together, declaring unity over the nation.

It was no longer about race or religion — it was about alignment with God's heart for South Africa.

The Cultural Economy

Gayton knew that preserving culture also meant empowering those who lived it.
    He introduced funding for small cultural businesses — from fashion designers to filmmakers.
    Festivals became opportunities not only to celebrate, but to create jobs.

Tourism boomed as South Africans and foreigners alike flocked to heritage routes — walking the paths of their ancestors, tasting traditional cuisine, and hearing the stories of the First Nation.

Culture was no longer a relic — it became currency.
    And it restored dignity to those who had long been forgotten.

The Spirit of Ubuntu Restored

The word Ubuntu — "I am because we are" — returned to the nation's vocabulary, not as a slogan, but as a way of life.

Communities began helping one another again.
   Street corners turned into gathering places for elders to tell stories.
   Neighbourhoods revived the tradition of sharing food, music, and laughter.

South Africans began to realize that culture is love made visible.
   And in that love, God's divine alignment began to unfold.

Closing Reflection

Culture is the mirror of a nation's soul.
   And when a people remember who they are, they remember Whose they are.

Through Gayton McKenzie's heart and leadership, South Africans rediscovered that they are not broken fragments of history — they are a tapestry woven by God's own design.

The Coloured child in Mitchell's Plain,
   The Zulu farmer in KwaZulu-Natal,
   The Xhosa mother in the Eastern Cape,
   The Koisan elder in the desert —
   All are threads of the same divine fabric.

The rebuilding of culture was not just about heritage — it was about healing.
   And as the nation danced, sang, and spoke its truth again, the words of the true patriot echoed across the land:

"When we honour our culture,
    we honour our Creator.
    And when we honour our Creator,
    we become one heart, one people, one nation — forever."

Chapter 18 — The Trials of the True Patriot

"Every true calling will be tested. Every true patriot will walk through fire — not to be destroyed, but to be refined."

The Weight of Leadership

Leadership is not a crown of gold — it is a cross of sacrifice.

When Gayton McKenzie accepted the responsibility to lead, to serve, and to heal, he knew it would not come without battle.

He once said,

"The moment you stand for truth, the enemy stands against you."

The more miracles he achieved, the louder the opposition became.

The more the nation began to unite, the more some forces tried to divide.

Because unity threatens those who profit from chaos.

Winds of Opposition

As the ministry flourished — rebuilding sports, reviving arts, and restoring culture — the critics grew restless.

Newspapers began spinning false stories.
Social media flooded with lies and twisted words.
Old enemies rose, disguised as friends.

They said he was arrogant.
They said he was dangerous.
They said he wanted power.

But they could not understand — he never wanted power; he wanted purpose.

Every headline designed to destroy his name only made his mission stronger.
He smiled and said,

"You cannot bury a seed that God Himself has planted."

The Battle of Truth

There came a time when political enemies tried to discredit his work.
They targeted his ministry, his faith, his friends.
They accused him of things he never said and crimes he never committed.

But Gayton did not fight with anger — he fought with integrity.
He opened the books.
He faced the people.
He spoke the truth openly.

In town halls, in interviews, and at rallies, he said:

"I serve God first, my people second, and myself last. If that offends anyone, so be it."

His transparency disarmed even his critics.

Because what can you say to a man who hides nothing?

The Lonely Road of Destiny

True patriots walk lonely roads.

When others sleep, they wrestle with the weight of their vision.

When others celebrate, they pray for strength.

Gayton often spent nights alone in reflection and prayer.

He carried the pain of his people like a father carries the pain of his children.

He prayed for wisdom, not victory.

For patience, not revenge.

For mercy, not glory.

Those who were close to him often said he had a lion's heart — strong, yet humble; fierce, yet forgiving.

The Voices of Division

There were those who tried to stir division within the movement — voices whispering lies, turning brothers against brothers, sowing confusion.

But Gayton reminded them of the foundation of the Patriotic Alliance: unity in diversity.

He said,

"If you break the chain of unity, you weaken the strength of the people."

He called for meetings of reconciliation — bringing together leaders, community members, and youth.

He reminded them that the struggle was not against each other, but against the forces that wanted to keep them divided and small.

That moment rekindled the fire of brotherhood — the fire of the aligned heart.

Standing Before the Storm

One day, a major newspaper published a story filled with lies and political manipulation.

It spread like wildfire, aiming to destroy his reputation and the work he was doing.

Social media exploded.

His opponents celebrated.

But Gayton did not respond with rage.

He stood before a crowd in Johannesburg and said:

"They write their lies in ink. I write my truth in people's hearts.

Paper burns, but the heart remembers."

The crowd erupted.

And for every false story printed, ten thousand people rose to defend him.

The truth began to travel faster than the lies.

Faith in the Fire

During his hardest days, Gayton turned to his faith.
He read Psalm 27:

"The Lord is my light and my salvation — whom shall I fear?
The Lord is the strength of my life — of whom shall I be afraid?"

He knew his purpose was greater than politics.
He was not just a leader — he was a messenger of alignment.
A man called to restore the pride, dignity, and unity of a forgotten nation.

Through betrayal, rejection, and attack, he stayed true to his calling.
Because true patriots are not defined by comfort — they are defined by character.

The Power of Resilience

The trials became his testimony.
The more they tried to destroy him, the more people saw his strength.
The more they tried to silence him, the more his voice became a chorus of the people.

He turned pain into purpose.
Criticism into courage.
And opposition into opportunity.

In the end, even some of his critics began to respect him — because they realized he was not pretending.
He was becoming.

The Nation's Response

Communities began holding prayer marches for him.
    Youth wrote songs titled "True Patriot."
    Artists painted murals of him surrounded by unity symbols — not as a politician, but as a symbol of courage and resilience.

He became the reflection of what every South African could be — strong, unshaken, and faithful in the face of adversity.

The Lesson of the Trials

Through the storms, Gayton learned — and taught — one of life's most powerful truths:

"The fire that tries to destroy you is the same fire that reveals what you're made of."

True patriotism is not proven in peace, but in pressure.
    Not in applause, but in accusation.
    Not in comfort, but in crisis.

And every trial became proof that his mission was divine.

Closing Reflection

In the end, the trials of the true patriot were not punishments — they were preparation.
    They revealed his strength, refined his faith, and united the people behind him.

He showed the nation that:

A true patriot does not seek fame — he seeks faithfulness.

A true patriot does not serve himself — he serves others.

A true patriot does not fear the storm — he becomes the calm within it.

Through fire, he was refined.
   Through hate, he was humbled.
   Through trial, he was aligned.

And South Africa saw — not just a leader —
   but the living example of The Heart of a True Patriot.

Chapter 19 — The People's Revival

"When one heart catches fire with purpose, it lights a thousand others."

The Awakening Begins

Revival does not begin in palaces — it begins in people.
Not in policies, but in hearts.

After years of division, corruption, and disappointment, something began to stir within the nation.
Men and women who had lost hope began to rise.
Communities once broken by violence and poverty began to rebuild themselves.

It was as if a spiritual wind swept across South Africa — calling people to remember who they were and what they were capable of.

And everywhere, one phrase was heard:

"Let's align with the heart of a true patriot."

The Spirit of Ownership

One of Gayton McKenzie's greatest teachings was that South Africans should stop waiting for government miracles and start becoming miracles themselves.

He said,

"Don't wait for someone to fix your street — paint it yourself.
Don't wait for a leader to save your child — be the leader."

And people listened.

In townships and rural villages, residents began cleaning their neighbourhoods, painting walls, and fixing playgrounds.

Youth groups planted trees.

Churches partnered with schools.

Small businesses began sponsoring community projects.

For the first time in years, people were not complaining — they were contributing.

The revival had begun.

Unity on the Ground

Communities that were once divided by race and class began working together.

In one Cape Town suburb, coloured and black families cleaned up a shared park together.

In the Northern Cape, elders and youth came together to restore a neglected heritage site.

It was no longer about who you were — it was about what you could build together.

The message of the movement spread through radio, schools, and churches:

"We are not enemies. We are family."

The Rise of the Young Patriots

The youth were the first to fully embrace the revival.
   They began calling themselves "The New Generation of Patriots."

High school students formed patriot clubs where they studied history, leadership, and self-discipline.
   College students organized volunteer programs in poor areas.
   Young artists wrote songs and poetry about unity, strength, and pride.

One teenage poet from Soweto said on stage:

"We are not lost children — we are the children of the soil,
   and we are rising to take back our nation."

That performance went viral, becoming a rallying cry for a generation tired of waiting for permission to dream.

The Church in Motion

Pastors, prophets, and spiritual leaders began preaching a new kind of message — not of fear, but of faith in action.
   They said revival was not just shouting "Amen" — it was showing up

to serve.

Churches began organizing community clean-ups, food drives, and mentorship programs.
  In some towns, Sunday services ended with congregations marching into the streets, cleaning, feeding, and restoring.

Gayton said,

"We cannot pray for change and ignore the pain.
  True prayer moves the hands to work and the heart to love."

Faith and action became one.
  Worship and work became inseparable.

The Church of the Aligned Heart had been born — not bound by walls, but free in the streets.

The Businessmen of Hope

Entrepreneurs began joining the movement too.
  They realized that true success meant giving back.
  Small and medium enterprises began sponsoring local sports teams, art programs, and school renovations.

Gayton launched the Patriotic Business Network, encouraging business owners to hire locally and invest in community growth.
  Instead of competing, they began collaborating.

For the first time, business became a bridge — not a barrier.

The Mothers of the Movement

No revival is complete without mothers.

In every township, it was the mothers who rose up — cooking, cleaning, organizing, and caring.

They became the backbone of the people's movement.

One grandmother in the Free State said,

"We have prayed enough — now we will do."

She and her friends started a feeding program that grew into a national campaign.

They called it "Heart of the Nation."

Soon, similar programs appeared everywhere — driven by ordinary women who refused to watch their communities decay.

They didn't wait for politics. They acted with love.

The Rebirth of Morality

As the revival spread, a sense of morality began to return.

People started speaking truth again.

Men took responsibility for their families.

Crime rates dropped in areas where communities united in faith and work.

Honesty became fashionable again.

Hard work was honoured again.

Prayer became powerful again.

The heart of the nation was beating differently — not with greed, but with grace.

Music of the Movement

Music once again became the anthem of the people's revival.
Choirs, street bands, and young artists began releasing songs about patriotism and purpose.

"We won't wait for heroes — we will become them.
We won't wait for freedom — we will live it.
We won't wait for change — we are the change."

The rhythms carried through taxis, radios, and schoolyards — the sound of a nation reborn.

The Return of Dignity

Dignity is not about wealth — it's about worth.
And for too long, South Africans had forgotten theirs.

Through Gayton's leadership and the movement he inspired, people began to lift their heads again.
Pride returned — not arrogance, but self-respect.
People began dressing neatly, walking tall, and speaking life over their children.

From homeless shelters to university halls, people began to declare:

"We are children of God, and we are South Africa — chosen and strong."

The Nation on Its Knees

In a historic moment, the movement organized a National Day of Prayer and Alignment.

Millions gathered in cities and villages, on beaches and fields, lifting their hands to heaven.

Different languages, different churches, different colours — one heart.
One purpose.
One prayer:

"Lord, align our hearts as one. Heal our land."

As the sun set that evening, choirs sang across the nation.
Some wept, others danced, but all felt one thing — unity.

The revival had become unstoppable.

Closing Reflection

The revival of the people was not a campaign — it was a calling.
It proved that patriotism is not about politics — it's about participation.
That love for your country begins with love for your neighbour.

From the richest cities to the poorest townships, one truth rang out:

"The power of a nation lies not in government, but in its people —
people who love, who build, who believe."

The people of South Africa had risen.

And through their unity, the prophecy was fulfilled —
The True Patriot had awakened a nation of patriots.

Chapter 20 — The Prophetic Alignment

"When heaven speaks, the earth must listen — and align."

The Whisper Before the Storm

Long before Gayton McKenzie rose to lead, before the Patriotic Alliance carried its green oacross the nation,
prophets in hidden places had already spoken.

They said,

"There will rise a man from the heart of the forgotten people,
who will not seek power, but purpose.
He will not come from privilege, but from pain.
He will carry the blood of the ancient ones,
and his voice will awaken the bones of a sleeping nation."

Those words sounded strange at the time — distant, almost poetic.
But years later, people would look back and say: "It was written."

The Ancient Promise

The Khoisan — the First People — carried more than just history; they carried prophecy.

Their bloodlines, mixed across generations, became the very DNA of South Africa's diversity.

They were the spiritual seed of unity — the bridge between all races.

When the prophecy spoke of "the man from the heart of the forgotten," many elders whispered, "He will come from among the Khoisan — the root of the land."

They believed that the rebirth of South Africa would not come from the powerful,

but from those who carried the heart of the soil — the ones who were counted out, but never erased.

The Sign of Alignment

When Gayton McKenzie became Minister of Sport, Arts and Culture, many said it was coincidence — politics.
But others saw something greater — confirmation.

His rise was not just a promotion.
It was alignment.

Everywhere he went, he carried restoration:
stadiums reopened, artists revived, sports federations healed, youth found hope again in places long forgotten.

The prophetic sign was clear — the heart of a true patriot had taken his rightful place,
not just in government, but in destiny.

The Nation at a Crossroad

Every prophecy requires a test.
Every promise meets resistance.

As Gayton's influence grew, so did the attacks.
Media storms. False reports. Political traps.
It seemed that darkness tried to drown out the light of purpose.

But those who had spiritual eyes understood:

"When destiny is about to manifest, opposition must rise — for light is proven by darkness."

Through every trial, he stood firm — focused, unshaken, his eyes fixed on God and his people.
That is when the prophets said,

"The alignment has begun."

The Prophets Speak Again

During this time, voices from across the land began to echo the same message.
From church pulpits to rural prayer circles, one phrase began to reappear:

"South Africa will be a light to the nations."

Prophets declared that the spirit of division was breaking,
that the rainbow would shine again — not as politics, but as prophecy

fulfilled.

And central to this vision was a rebirth of the heart.
A return to the values of love, honour, truth, and work.

They said,

"God is raising patriots — not politicians.
Builders — not blamers.
Servants — not seekers of power."

The Dream Vision

One night, a respected elder from the Northern Cape had a vision.
He saw a great heart beating over the land —
its veins stretching from Cape Town to Limpopo, from Durban to Upington.

Each pulse of the heart sent waves of light through towns and villages.
Wherever the light touched, people stood up —
some crying, some praying, some lifting their hands to the sky.

And in the center of the heart was written:

"Alignment of the Hearts — The True Patriot."

The elder woke with tears and said,

"This is not about one man. It's about a movement of hearts aligned with Heaven."

The Spiritual Connection

Patriotism without purpose becomes pride.
    But when it connects with divine will, it becomes prophecy fulfilled.

That is what was happening in South Africa —
    a nation rediscovering its divine purpose,
    realizing that unity was never man's idea,
    but God's design.

It was written in the colours of the land,
    in the diversity of its people,
    in the rhythm of its languages.

The rainbow was never political — it was prophetic.

The Fire of Intercession

As revival spread, so did intercession.
    Prayer meetings erupted in schools, stadiums, and prisons.
    People prayed not for power — but for purity of purpose.

In one unforgettable night in Pretoria,
    thousands knelt on the grass and prayed as one:

"Lord, align our hearts with Yours."

The heavens seemed to respond — a sudden breeze swept through the
crowd,
    and some said they heard a sound like a heartbeat in the wind.

That night became known as The Night of Alignment.
  It marked a spiritual turning point for the nation.

The Prophetic Symbols

Signs began to follow:

Rain falling over drought-stricken towns after community prayers.

Sports teams that united across divisions and won together.

Artists producing songs that healed old wounds.

Families reconciling after decades of separation.

Each act became a symbol — not random, but revealing.
  The people were not just living history; they were fulfilling prophecy.

The Role of the True Patriot

A true patriot, as Gayton had always taught,
  is not defined by flag or party,
  but by love and responsibility.

He said,

"A true patriot serves without expecting reward,
  builds without demanding credit,
  and fights not to be remembered — but to make others live better."

That heart — humble, bold, aligned —

was the very heart the prophecy spoke of.

And through his obedience, the prophecy of alignment began to take form.

The National Covenant

Soon, spiritual leaders across the nation gathered to declare a new covenant —
   a promise between God and the people of South Africa.

They declared:

"We, the people of this land, dedicate our hearts to unity,
   our hands to service,
   our voices to truth,
   and our lives to love."

It was not written by politicians,
   but prayed by patriots.

And from that day, South Africa was marked —
   a nation under divine realignment.

The Heavenly Alignment

The final prophecy was simple but perfect:

"As the hearts of the people align,
   heaven will align with the land."

That alignment began to manifest — not in the skies, but in everyday life.

In forgiveness.

In community.

In national pride reborn through humility.

And those who once doubted began to believe —

not in a party,

not in a leader,

but in the divine calling upon the nation itself.

Closing Reflection

Prophecy is not prediction — it is partnership.

It calls, and we respond.

The alignment of the hearts was not an accident; it was a divine appointment.

The rise of the true patriot was not luck; it was destiny unfolding.

As Gayton once said in a speech that echoed across the land:

"The true patriot is the one who loves enough to serve,

believes enough to build,

and prays enough to stay humble."

And in that alignment — between heaven and earth, faith and action —

South Africa stepped into her divine destiny.

The Obedient Patriot — Fulfillment of the Prophecy

There comes a time when a man stops walking by sight and begins walking fully by faith. For Gayton McKenzie, that moment had been written in Heaven long before he was born. A prophecy once went out over his life — that he would one day go far around the world, gather the dry, dead bones of his people buried in foreign lands, and bring them home.

This was not only a physical mission, but a spiritual restoration. The bones represented the identity, pride, and heritage of a people forgotten by history, yet remembered by God.

When the time came, he did not resist the calling. He became obedient to the prophecy. As Minister of Sport, Arts and Culture, he did what others tried to do for more than thirty years — and he accomplished it within one year of stepping into office.

He united names, memories, and legacies — putting together the statuses of his people alongside those who once fought, were imprisoned, and even died for freedom on Robben Island. The once-forgotten children of the soil were remembered again, and their story restored to the heart of South Africa.

Where others saw division, Gayton saw destiny. Where others delayed, he delivered. That is the mark of a true patriot — one who obeys God before man, one who fulfills the prophecy no matter the cost.

Even in sport, where entire traditions were once silenced and banned, he reopened the gates. A sport that was once declared illegal — one that lived deeply in the hearts of his people — became legal and celebrated again. It was not just a victory for a community; it was the restoration of joy, identity, and belonging.

Through every action, Gayton McKenzie lived out what God had spoken long ago. He became the bridge between prophecy and reality, between history and tomorrow. He brought home not only bones — but hope, pride, and divine alignment.

In the hands of a true patriot, prophecy becomes promise fulfilled. And that is what Gayton McKenzie has done — not for himself, but for God, for his people, and for the generations to come. A man Called to be a leader and create leaders.

Chapter 21 — The Battle for Truth

"When lies become louder, truth must shine brighter."

The Calm Before the Clash

Every great movement of light eventually meets the shadow.
When hearts align for good, darkness grows desperate.

The revival had reached every corner of South Africa.
Communities were working together, people were inspired,
and faith was blooming where despair once lived.

But behind closed doors, another story was being written —
a story of resistance, jealousy, and deception.

The battle had shifted from the streets to the airwaves,
from communities to the media —
from hearts to headlines.

The War of Words

It began slowly — whispers, rumours, manipulated reports.

Then suddenly, the air was filled with noise.

Talk shows questioned motives.
Newspapers twisted truth.
Social media fed on division.

They painted Gayton McKenzie as a man of controversy,
a "problem," a "populist," even a "danger."

But those who knew the truth, who had seen his heart,
saw something else —
they saw a man being tested for purpose.

One pastor said,

"If you are not attacked, you are not advancing."

The Test of Character

It would have been easy to fight back with anger,
to respond blow for blow.
But Gayton remained still — calm, focused, unshaken.

He knew that no lie lasts forever,
and no truth dies quietly.

He said to his team one day,

"Let them speak. Let them write. Let them twist.
The truth doesn't need protection — it only needs time."

Those words became a mantra for the movement.
  Truth would defend itself.

The Weapon of Integrity

During those turbulent months, Gayton kept doing what he was called
to do:
  building, serving, uplifting.

He opened sports academies in poor towns,
  funded art projects for youth,
  and restored abandoned heritage sites.

Each act of goodness became a counterattack against lies.
  He didn't fight with anger — he fought with action.

And the people saw.
  They began to say,

"The papers can lie, but the man cannot."

The Voice of the People

Something incredible happened —
  ordinary citizens began to rise in defence of truth.

On social media, in church gatherings, in taxi ranks and schools,
  people began speaking up:

"We know his heart. We've seen his work. We stand with him."

They posted videos of restored sports fields,
    photos of schoolchildren with art kits,
    clips of community events revived under his ministry.

The narrative began to shift.
    The people became the journalists of truth.

The Spiritual Warfare

But behind the physical storm was something deeper —
    a spiritual battle.

Prayer warriors and intercessors began to sense the heaviness in the air.
    They gathered in prayer, fasting, declaring Psalm 91 and Ephesians 6 over the nation.

They prayed:

"No weapon formed against truth shall prosper.
    Every tongue that rises against the righteous shall fall."

And slowly, the atmosphere began to change.
    The noise started fading.
    The truth began to surface.

The Moment of Revelation

Then came the day of exposure.

A journalist who had worked on one of the hit pieces came forward

publicly,
confessing that much of the story had been fabricated under pressure.

He said,

"I wrote things I knew weren't true.
I saw a man with purpose, but I was told to paint him as a problem."

That confession became national news —
and suddenly, the lies began to crumble like dust.

People saw the bigger picture:
This was not just a political fight —
it was a spiritual war over the heart of a nation.

Standing Firm

When Gayton was asked by reporters for a response, he smiled and said simply,

"Let truth speak for itself."

No revenge. No bitterness.
Just peace — the kind only a true patriot carries.

He reminded the nation,

"We cannot heal the country with hate.
We can only build it with truth."

His calmness disarmed critics,

and his integrity silenced accusations.

The Awakening of Discernment

The battle for truth opened the eyes of millions.
    People began questioning what they believed,
    checking facts, and seeking deeper understanding.

The nation was learning discernment —
    a gift that would guard it for generations.

Churches began hosting workshops on media literacy and truth in public life.
    Schools introduced lessons on ethics and integrity.
    The movement had sparked a national hunger for honesty.

Truth had not just survived — it had multiplied.

The Light Through the Cracks

It is said that light enters through the cracks of a broken vessel.
    And in the cracks of controversy, South Africa found clarity.

The false stories only made the real story stronger —
    a story of a man who refused to be moved by slander,
    and a nation that refused to be manipulated by fear.

Truth stood up, and lies fell down.

The Voice of Heaven

Prophets across the nation began declaring that the storm was ending.
  They said,

"God has tested the heart of His servant and proven his calling."

They compared Gayton's journey to that of Joseph —
  betrayed, misunderstood, yet destined for greatness.

For even in the pit of false accusation,
  his purpose only grew clearer.

The Rebirth of Trust

Out of the ashes of deception came something unexpected — trust.

People began trusting again — not in politicians,
  but in values: honesty, service, faith, and love.

The media, too, began to shift.
  A few brave journalists launched a new initiative called "The Truth
Table,"
  dedicated to fair, honest reporting on national transformation.

The fire of lies had purified the land.

Closing Reflection

Every true patriot must one day face the battle for truth.
  It is the fire that reveals the gold within.

Through persecution came purification.

Through resistance came revelation.
Through slander came strength.

As Gayton said to a gathering of youth in that season:

"Don't fight lies with hate — fight them with excellence.
Don't let darkness define you — let your light expose it."

And so, the battle for truth became a victory for alignment.
For when the hearts of a people are aligned with God and grounded in truth —
no lie can ever stand against them.

Chapter 22 — The Rebuilding of the Nation

"A nation is not rebuilt with money or laws — it is rebuilt with hearts that refuse to give up."

The Dawn After the Darkness

Every storm, no matter how fierce, ends with sunrise.

After the chaos, the noise, the lies, and the attacks — peace began to settle over South Africa.

The people had endured the battle for truth, and they emerged stronger, wiser, and more united than ever before.

It was as if the country had taken a deep breath after years of suffocation.

The air felt lighter.

The streets felt safer.

And hope, once buried, began to bloom again.

It was time to rebuild — not just buildings and systems, but the soul of the nation.

The Vision of Renewal

Gayton McKenzie stepped forward once again — not as a politician, but as a servant.

He called for a National Rebuilding Campaign, saying,

"We cannot change the past, but we can repair the future."

His first move was to unite the ministries of Sport, Arts, and Culture under one goal:

to restore dignity through creativity, discipline, and pride.

Sports brought discipline.

Arts brought expression.

Culture brought identity.

Together, they became the foundation of national healing.

Sport as a Seed of Unity

Under his leadership, neglected sports facilities reopened.

Abandoned stadiums were revived and filled with life again.

Grassroots programs began sprouting across provinces, bringing hope to forgotten towns.

Young athletes received proper coaching, equipment, and recognition.

Communities rallied around local teams, cheering not only for victory, but for unity.

One of Gayton's most famous lines during this era was:

"When a child holds a ball, he drops the weapon."

Sport became the heartbeat of reconciliation.

Black, white, coloured, Indian — on the field, they were all South Africans.

The Arts Rise Again

Art, music, and storytelling began to thrive once more.

The Ministry launched The True Patriot Creative Fund — empowering young artists, poets, musicians, and filmmakers to tell their own stories.

Instead of importing foreign influences, South Africa began celebrating its own.

Documentaries about Khoisan heritage filled television screens.

Schoolchildren painted murals of unity and rebirth.

Musicians collaborated across genres, mixing languages and sounds into a national symphony of pride.

As one young artist said at a festival,

"We are not just painting pictures — we are painting our future."

Culture as the Core

Gayton often said,

"If we lose our culture, we lose our compass."

So he made it his mission to revive the cultural heartbeat of the nation.

Traditional music, dance, and festivals received new funding and attention.

Heritage sites were restored with respect and purpose.
The history of the Khoisan and other indigenous groups was rewritten — truthfully this time — in school textbooks.

Cultural pride was no longer a memory. It became a movement.

Education and Empowerment

Rebuilding the nation meant educating it.
So the ministry partnered with schools, NGOs, and churches to teach patriotism not as politics, but as purpose.

Workshops were held titled "The Heart of a True South African."
Youth learned the values of responsibility, service, and pride.
Teachers were trained to inspire rather than simply instruct.

In universities, students debated the meaning of modern patriotism.
In villages, elders shared oral history around fires.

The young and the old began to walk hand in hand again.

The New Generation of Builders

The youth who once felt forgotten were now leading the charge.
They volunteered to clean parks, paint schools, plant trees, and mentor younger kids.

They began to call themselves "The Builders of Tomorrow."
Their slogan was simple:

"If it's broken, we fix it."

Across provinces, you could see green shirts with the word Patriot printed on the back — young people wearing hope with pride.

What began as one man's dream had become a generation's mission.

Women at the Foundation

Women were the glue that held the rebuilding together.
   Gayton often honoured them publicly, saying,

"The mothers of our land are the architects of our future."

From feeding schemes to mentorship programs, from art projects to business ventures — women led with strength and compassion.
   They transformed communities through love that expected no credit.

In rural areas, women's cooperatives began producing crafts, textiles, and traditional food products — selling locally and internationally.
   Their slogan: "Made with Heart in South Africa."

The nation was being rebuilt, one heart at a time — and many of those hearts were women's.

The Return of Honour

One of the most powerful transformations was moral.
   Honour returned — to families, to workplaces, to leadership.

Corruption began to lose its grip as communities held leaders accountable.
   People started celebrating honesty again.

A handshake regained meaning.
A promise became sacred once more.

Gayton said in one of his speeches,

"Honour is the unseen architecture of every strong nation."

And soon, honour became fashionable again.

The Healing of the Land

Rebuilding went beyond infrastructure — it extended to nature itself.
Environmental programs began restoring rivers, cleaning coastlines,
and planting millions of trees.
Each project was tied to the theme of alignment:

"As we heal our land, our land heals us."

Communities prayed before planting,
sang while cleaning rivers,
and danced when the first green shoots appeared.

It wasn't just environmental — it was spiritual.

The Miracle of Employment

Through creative industries and community rebuilding, thousands
found jobs.
But more importantly — they found purpose.

Small businesses flourished, not through handouts, but through partnership.

Workshops trained people in carpentry, construction, event management, and cultural tourism.

The unemployed became builders of hope.

For the first time in years, unemployment began to drop not because of government programs — but because of people's passion.

The Return of Joy

Something beautiful began to happen — laughter returned.

Music filled the air again.

Children played freely.

People greeted one another in the streets.

The national mood shifted from survival to celebration.

The flag was not just flown — it was felt.

People were proud to say,

"I am South African — and I belong here."

Faith and the Future

Churches became centers of rebuilding too — offering skills training, counselling, and mentorship.

They didn't just pray for revival; they built it.

Pastors preached messages of alignment and accountability.

They reminded their congregations that the heart of a true patriot beats with both prayer and action.

Faith had become not just belief, but blueprint.

Closing Reflection

Rebuilding a nation is not about cement or policies.
   It's about healing the invisible fractures within people's hearts.

Through faith, truth, and unity, South Africa began to rise — not as a divided collection of tribes, but as one family under God.

As Gayton said during the National Day of Unity:

"We have seen our brokenness — and we have chosen to build again.
   The world will look at South Africa and say:
   'That is what alignment looks like.'"

The true patriot had done what few could —
   he turned pain into purpose,
   and history into hope.

Chapter 23 — The Global Witness

"When a nation is healed, its light does not stay hidden — it becomes a beacon for others."

The World Begins to Watch

News travels fast — but truth travels deeper.

After years of struggle and realignment, the transformation happening in South Africa could no longer be ignored.
Foreign media outlets began to notice something remarkable:
crime rates dropping, communities rebuilding, youth volunteering, and churches leading national renewal.

They called it "The South African Turnaround."
Others called it "The Miracle of the South."

But those who lived through it knew it wasn't luck — it was alignment.
The alignment of hearts, vision, and faith.

From Division to Demonstration

For decades, South Africa had been a symbol of division — of apartheid, corruption, and pain.

But now, the world was witnessing a new story unfold.

Once, other nations sent missionaries and aid to South Africa.

Now, South Africa began sending out ambassadors of hope.

Teams of youth, artists, and spiritual leaders travelled to neighbouring countries — Mozambique, Botswana, Namibia, Zimbabwe — carrying a message of unity and empowerment.

They didn't go with money or speeches; they went with testimonies.

One young leader told a crowd in Lusaka,

"We are not here to show off our progress.

We are here to show you what happens when a nation forgives itself."

The world listened — and believed.

The Speech That Changed the World

Gayton McKenzie was invited to speak at the United Nations Global Forum for Leadership and Ethics in Geneva.

It was his first international appearance since the rebuilding began.

He stood before presidents, ambassadors, and leaders from across the globe and said:

"We were once the nation of struggle.

We became the nation of survival.

But now we are the nation of strength.

We learned that leadership is not domination — it is service.
  We learned that unity is not agreement — it is alignment.

The time has come for nations to stop competing in pride,
  and start collaborating in purpose."

When he finished, the entire hall rose to its feet.
  For several minutes, the applause did not stop.
  Tears streamed down the faces of leaders who had only known South Africa through headlines of pain.
  Now they were witnessing the rebirth of a people.

A Model for the World

Soon, global think tanks and universities began studying the South African Model of Alignment.
  It was not a political theory — it was a spiritual reality translated into governance.

They documented how the Ministry of Sport, Arts, and Culture had become the engine of national healing.
  How churches and communities had partnered with government.
  How truth had replaced propaganda, and unity had replaced fear.

The phrase "Alignment Governance" began appearing in academic papers, leadership seminars, and even UN training sessions.

For the first time, South Africa wasn't a case study in failure —
  it was a blueprint for redemption.

The Rise of Global Partnerships

Countries that once ignored Africa began to seek partnerships.
Not for resources, but for wisdom.

Delegations came from as far as Japan, Brazil, and Norway to learn from the new South Africa.
They visited community centres, youth academies, and art festivals.
They met with village leaders, pastors, and young entrepreneurs.

One Japanese diplomat said,

"You have taught us that innovation begins with compassion."

Global organizations began funding South African projects — not as charity, but as collaboration.
They wanted to be part of something real.

The United Hearts Declaration

In 2031, South Africa hosted the World Congress of Unity and Renewal in Cape Town.
Leaders from over 80 nations attended.
During this historic gathering, Gayton McKenzie and spiritual leaders from around the world signed a document known as the United Hearts Declaration.

It stated:

"We, the nations of the earth, commit to lead not through power,
but through purpose.
We commit to heal before we build,
to serve before we rule,

and to align before we advance."

It became the moral constitution of a new global awakening.

The Rise of African Leadership

For the first time in modern history, Africa wasn't following — it was leading.
From Ghana to Kenya, Nigeria to Rwanda, countries began adopting the Alignment Principle.

African leaders started speaking not from bitterness, but from brilliance.
They saw that leadership with heart could change more than economies — it could change destinies.

The African Union launched the "Pan-African Alignment Initiative" — a plan for shared values, trade, and unity inspired by South Africa's transformation.

The slogan read:

"Africa: One Vision, Many Nations, Aligned in Heart."

The Cultural Export

Beyond politics and policy, South African art became the language of the new movement.

Music from Cape Town, poetry from Soweto, films from Johannesburg — all carried a spiritual frequency of pride, healing, and purpose.
Amapiano and gospel fused into a global rhythm of renewal.

Festivals in London, Toronto, and Dubai featured South African artists who sang not only of love, but of destiny.

Everywhere they went, they shared the same message:

"We are proof that God still restores nations."

The Return of the Pilgrims

Tourists and believers from all over the world began to visit South Africa — not for safaris or beaches, but for spiritual pilgrimage.

They came to see where it all began —
   the prayer movements, the rebuilding campaigns, the community miracles.

Churches that once sent missionaries to Africa were now sending groups to learn from Africa.

Cape Town became known as "The City of Alignment."
   Johannesburg — "The City of Hearts."
   And South Africa as a whole — "The Lighthouse of the South."

The True Patriotic Message

In a televised world address, Gayton McKenzie summarized the heart of the movement:

"We did not rebuild our nation by fighting each other.
   We rebuilt it by aligning with God and serving one another.

Our story is not about perfection — it's about redemption.
   And every nation that chooses humility and truth will rise again."

Those words were translated into 42 languages and shared worldwide.
   For weeks, social media trended with the hashtag #AlignmentOf-Hearts.

The Ripple of Revival

Within years, other nations began to witness their own awakenings.
   Brazil launched a National Day of Reconciliation.
   India began community rebuilding through art and culture.
   Even in Europe and the Americas, young people started movements focused on spiritual and national alignment.

It was no longer a South African revival —
   it was a global revolution of the heart.

The Legacy of the True Patriot

In the closing years of his public life, Gayton McKenzie often reflected quietly:

"I was just one voice.
   But one voice, aligned with truth, can echo across generations."

He had become more than a leader —
   he was a symbol of what God can do with a willing heart.

And as he stepped back from politics to focus on mentorship and ministry, the people carried forward his mission.

The movement no longer needed one man.
It had become a living heartbeat within every believer, every builder, every patriot.

Final Reflection

From the pain of division to the power of alignment,
from national struggle to global influence —
South Africa had become a testimony to the world.

Not because it was perfect,
but because it was willing to heal.

As the world watched, one truth became undeniable:

"When hearts align with God, nations rise again."

And so, The True Patriot story did not end in South Africa —
it began there.
A nation reborn became a world restored.

Chapter 24: The Dawn of Alignment

There comes a moment in every nation's story when time itself pauses.

When history bends toward destiny, and the hearts of its people begin to beat as one.

For South Africa, that moment is now.

From the forgotten corners of our townships to the glittering lights of our cities, a quiet revolution has begun — not one of violence or anger, but one of alignment.

Hearts are awakening.

Minds are renewing.

Dreams once buried are being dug up again, shining with hope and faith.

This movement — the spirit of true patriotism — was never about politics or power.

It was about people.

It was about rediscovering the soul of a nation that had been wounded, divided, and doubted.

And through all the storms, one truth has stood firm:

The heart of South Africa still beats strong.

A Nation Reawakened

The people have begun to see what it means to love their country again.

To take pride in their heritage, to defend their culture, and to build bridges where walls once stood.

From every background, from every race, from every faith — the call of the True Patriot is echoing across the land.

They no longer ask, "What can South Africa do for me?"

They now ask, "What can I do for South Africa?"

That is the heartbeat of the new generation — the alignment of hearts that the prophets once spoke of, the revival that God promised would come.

The True Patriot's Example

When Gayton McKenzie rose to lead — not as a politician, but as a servant of the people — something shifted.

His story became more than his own; it became a mirror for millions.

He showed that no past is too broken for purpose, and no dream too distant for destiny.

As Minister of Sport, Arts and Culture, he reminded us that sport is not only competition — it's unity.

That art is not just expression — it's healing.

That culture is not about separation — it's identity.

He opened doors for forgotten artists.

He empowered communities to rebuild their own pride.

He gave young athletes hope again, reminding them that their dreams were part of a greater national story.

And though critics tried to break him, though newspapers twisted truth and enemies whispered lies, he stood tall — because his heart was anchored in purpose.

He did not fight for praise; he fought for people.

He did not speak for power; he spoke for peace.

That is the mark of a true patriot.

The Final Alignment

The alignment of the hearts is not just a political awakening — it is a spiritual rebirth.

It is when love replaces bitterness.

When unity replaces division.

When forgiveness becomes stronger than fear.

For centuries, the Khoisan people — the First Nation — carried the burden of forgotten history.

But now, they rise as the foundation of renewal.

Their story, once silenced, is now part of South Africa's heartbeat again.

Their blood, their wisdom, and their resilience have become the roots from which a new patriotism grows — one that includes every South African.

In this divine alignment, the past and future meet.

The pain becomes purpose.

The struggle becomes strength.

And the people, once divided, become one nation under God.

A Call to Every South African

To be a true patriot is to carry love even when it hurts.
It is to serve without expecting recognition.
It is to believe in your nation when others have lost faith.

It is to wake up each morning and say:

"I will build, not break.
I will unite, not divide.
I will love, not hate."

That is the call of the aligned heart.
That is the legacy we leave for the next generation.

South Africa's destiny is not behind her — it is before her.
And as long as there are men and women willing to love her, protect her, and believe in her future, this land will rise again.

Final Words

The dawn has come.
The hearts have aligned.
The true patriots are rising.

From Cape Town to Limpopo, from Gqeberha to Kimberly — a new chapter has begun.
A nation reborn through courage, unity, and divine purpose.

Let this be our declaration:

We are one people.
We are one nation.
We are the heart of Africa —
And we are the True Patriots.

THE TRUE PATRIOT: A CALL TO SOUTH AFRICA'S YOUTH AND FUTURE LEADERS

By Shane Marquin van Rooyen

In every generation, there comes a book that is more than words — it becomes a **mirror of the nation's soul**.

The True Patriot: Alignment of the Hearts is such a book.

It speaks not only to the mind but to the heart of every South African — reminding us who we are, where we come from, and what kind of country we can still become.

This book was written with one vision:

To awaken the spirit of **true patriotism** — not as politics, but as **purpose**.

It is a message to the *youth*, the *dreamers*, the *workers*, the *leaders*, and the *forgotten*.

It is a message to those who still believe that the destiny of South Africa can be shaped by hands of courage, love, and faith.

WHY THIS BOOK MATTERS

South Africa is a land of promise.

But that promise can only be fulfilled when the hearts of its people begin to **align** — when we remember that we are one nation, born from different roots but destined for the same future.

This book carries the story of resilience — from the ancient Khoisan bloodlines that first walked this land, to the modern generation that still carries their spirit of endurance.

It celebrates **the coloured nation**, the *First People of the land*, whose pain and pride are woven into the soil of our history.

It reminds us that unity is not built on skin colour — it is built on **character** and **commitment**.

It tells the story of **Gayton McKenzie**, a man who rose from struggle to leadership, who became the voice of the voiceless and a living example of a **True Patriot**.

Through his life, we see what it means to love a nation beyond words — to serve with purpose, to fight for dignity, and to stand for truth even when the world stands against you.

MY AFRICAN DREAM — THE SONG THAT PROPHESIED THE FUTURE

Years ago, a woman wrote a song — and she sang it with the fire of faith.

Her name is **Vicky Sampson**, and her song was called **"My African Dream."**

It was not just a melody.

It was not just lyrics.

It was a *prophecy*.

In that song lived the heartbeat of a continent and the whisper of God's promise to His people:

"Let it be that my African dream will soon come true."

Today, that dream walks hand in hand with the **prophecy given to the Minister**,

for this is the time of **alignment**, the time of **fulfillment**.

Through leadership that honours God and uplifts people,

South Africa begins to sing that same song again — not only with voices, but with hearts united in purpose.

FOR THE YOUTH — THE LEADERS OF TOMORROW

To the youth of South Africa:

You are not the lost generation — you are the *chosen generation*.

You carry in your hearts the power to rewrite the story of this nation.

But before you can lead others, you must first **know who you are**.

That is what this book teaches.

The True Patriot is not a textbook — it is a guide, a mirror, a mentor in written form.

It teaches that leadership begins with **the heart**, not the title.

It shows that a true patriot is not the loudest in words but the strongest in love.

It challenges young people to rise — not to destroy, but to build.

Not to fight each other, but to fight for each other.

If you read this book, you will see that your history is not a curse — it is your crown.

And your voice, when aligned with truth, can shake mountains.

FOR EVERY SOUTH AFRICAN

Whether you are a teacher, a parent, a pastor, a student, or a worker — this book speaks to *you*.

It calls you to look deeper, to rediscover your faith in this land, and to understand that **South Africa's healing begins with us**.

We cannot wait for others to save our nation — we must become the saviours of our own time.

Every child we inspire, every family we strengthen, every truth we stand for — is a step toward the rebirth of this country.

The True Patriot: Alignment of the Hearts is more than a book — it is a **movement of awakening**.

It is a vision of a South Africa where every citizen, no matter their colour or background, stands side by side and says:

> *"This is our home.*
> *This is our time.*
> *And we will protect it with love, courage, and truth."*

A GODLY CALL – NOT JUST FOR OURSELVES

We don't do it only for ourselves — we do it because it is a **Godly call**.

We serve not for recognition, but for **obedience** to the One who placed purpose within our hearts.

We do it **for God**, and that is why we, as **True Patriots**, will always put **God first**.

This message will be known for **generations to come** —

for it is not built on pride, but on prayer.

Not on politics, but on **principle**.

Not on human power, but on **divine purpose**.

Our mission is clear:

To rebuild this nation from the inside out — heart by heart, soul by soul.

Because when we honour God, we restore the land.

And when we stand together as True Patriots, **nothing can divide us again.**

Salut!

To God be the Glory — *for South Africa, forever free.*

Written *By Shane Marquin van Rooyen*

Author of *The True Patriot: Alignment of the Hearts*

Founder — Open Door Evangelism and Outreach Ministry South Africa

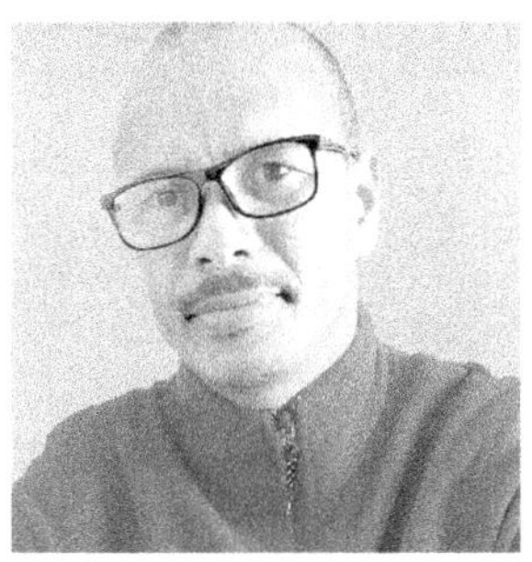

About the Author

Shane Marquin van Rooyen is a visionary leader, author, and founder of **The Open Door Evangelism & Outreach Ministry South Africa** — a movement devoted to uplifting communities, spreading hope, and realigning hearts with God's purpose.

Born from the vibrant heritage of the **Coloured Nation**, the descendants of the **Khoisan people**, Shane carries within him the ancient rhythm of Africa's first custodians — a spirit of endurance, faith, and unity.

His journey, shaped by trials and triumphs, has led him to become a voice for the voiceless and a beacon of restoration in a nation hungry for healing.

As a writer, Shane blends **faith, purpose, and patriotism** into a message that transcends politics and speaks straight to the soul.

Through his works — including *The True Patriot: Alignment of the Hearts* — he calls South Africans to remember their divine identity, to honour their roots, and to walk boldly in alignment with God's vision for their lives and their land.

He believes that a **True Patriot** is not defined by colour, wealth, or status, but by a heart willing to serve God and humanity.

With every word he writes and every outreach he leads, Shane reminds us that unity is possible, hope is alive, and destiny is real.

Beyond writing, Shane is the driving force behind **Shane's Books** and the creative label **Go Viral**, platforms where faith meets art, and vision becomes movement.

His life and message continue to inspire leaders, believers, and dreamers to rise — not for themselves, but for the generations to come.

"I write not for fame or applause,

but to awaken a nation.

For when true patriots align,

God's purpose is fulfilled."

— *Shane Marquin van Rooyen*